# EXPERIMENTING
## WITH
# COLOR

*BY KURT NASSAU*

A VENTURE BOOK

FRANKLIN WATTS A Division of Grolier Publishing
New York • London • Hong Kong • Sydney • Danbury, Connecticut

Photographs ©: Fundamental Photos: 73, 79 (Richard Megna); Kurt Nassau: 67, 93, 94, 95, 97; Omni-Photo Communications: 23 (Andy Deering), 1, 101 (Alice Grulich-Jones); Peter Arnold Inc.: 29, 33, 69, 98 (Leonard Lessin); Photo Researchers: 10 (Gordon Garradd/SPL), 56 (Renee Lynn), 76 (Pekka Parviainen/SPL), 61 (Sinclair Stammers/SPL); Smithsonian Institution: 107; Tony Stone Images: 7 (John Beatty), 75 (Chad Ehlers).
Illustrations created by Vantage Art

Library of Congress Cataloging-in-Publication Data

Nassau, Kurt
    Experimenting with color / Kurt Nassau
    p.     cm.
    Includes bibliographical references and index.
    Summary: Experiments and activities reinforce a general discussion of the properties of light, the electromagnetic spectrum, and color vision, that also outlines the fifteen ways in which electron interactions result in color.
    ISBN 0-531-11327-2
    1. Color—Juvenile literature. [1. Color.] I. Title.
QC495.5.N37 1997
535.6-dc20                                                          96-25865
                                                                        CIP
                                                                         AC

# EXPERIMENTING
## WITH
## COLOR

# CONTENTS

# INTRODUCTION
## THE WHY OF COLOR

L ook around your living room at dusk, when it is so dark that you can hardly see. You can see a cat jump off the sofa, but is it the gray cat or the ginger one? You can see the size and shape of the chairs, the sofa, and the tables. You can even see that the couch has a pattern on it, that the walls are bright and the rug is dark, but what are the colors? Everything is gray and black— monotonously drab.

When you turn on a light, everything changes. Suddenly the whole world of color opens up. You see pastel shades of sky blue and grass green, tints of yellow and brown, and highlights of fire-engine red, brilliant turquoise, and intense royal blue. Do this experiment and you will see the world differently. You will gain insight into color—one of the wonders of the universe that we usually just take for granted.

What is this thing called color? Where does it come from? How do we see it? You will find the answers to these and many other questions in this book.

The ice in glaciers appears blue because the water molecules in the ice vibrate and absorb a little light at the red end of the visible spectrum.

## MYTHS ABOUT COLOR

I have just returned from a trip to Alaska, where I saw lots of glaciers. A tour guide told us that glaciers are blue because the extreme cold changes the structure of the ice. Another guide told us that the oceans are blue because they reflect the blue of the sky. At one time, these explanations were believed to be true, but we now have a much better understanding of the real reason for these two colors, as you will see in Chapter 4.

We first learn about color when we are very young and are not yet ready for all the details. Later in life we are surprised to realize that we do not really understand what causes the colors we see every day. For example, there are actually several sets of *primary colors,* not just the set that consists of red, yellow, and blue. And you may be surprised to discover that mixing the colors used in painting is quite different from mixing the colors used in lighting for the stage.

## HOW WE SEE COLOR

Sight is the most important of our senses. We learn most of what we know about our world through our eyes. We see the world as shapes, sizes, distances, and movements. In addition, our eyes can distinguish about 10 million different colors. The Earth is lit up by the sun, so our idea of "white" comes from sunlight. However, white light from the sun is actually made up of all the colors we see in the rainbow.

If some of these colors are removed from white light, the remaining light is no longer white—it is colored. This is what happens when you look at a red sunset, an orange carrot, yellow gold, green grass, or a blue sky. We can also see color created by light emitted from other light sources: the yellow light of a candle flame, the beam of a red laser, or the blue light of a mercury-vapor lamp.

Why is grass green? We can say that grass is green because it reflects the green light that is present in white daylight, and absorbs the other colors. Grass contains a substance called *chlorophyll*. Electrons in the chlorophyll absorb all of the colors that make up white light—except green.

The chapters that follow will explain how and why we see color all around us. Along the way you will explore the nature of light, find out what color is, learn how we see color, and come to understand the curiosities of color mixing. Some chemical formulas are given for those of you who know a little chemistry. If these mean nothing to you, don't worry—just ignore them.

It is easy and fun to make the observations and do the experiments described in this book. You will learn about the many interesting and unexpected properties of color. You may even come up with ideas about how to design experiments of your own.

## A NOTE ABOUT SAFETY

1. Experiment only under the supervision of a teacher or other knowledgeable adult.

2. Always read the instructions right to the end and make sure you understand them before starting an experiment.

3. Never look at the sun without wearing very dark sunglasses or two pairs of ordinary sunglasses.

4. Be careful when experimenting with flames or hot objects. Remember that lightbulbs can get very hot.

5. Discuss your ideas for new experiments with an adult before trying them.

The spectral colors of the rainbow are produced by dispersion in drops of rain.

# CHAPTER ONE
## RAINBOWS, SUNDOGS, AND THE FIRE IN GEMSTONES

Have you ever seen a rainbow in the sky when the sun shines during a rain shower? You can also see a rainbow in a glass of water or in the spray from a garden hose. Exploring rainbows will help you understand that white light is made up of all the colors of the *spectrum*, as well as other things. As you will see, both *refraction* and *dispersion* are at work. These same effects also explain sundogs and the "fire" in gemstones.

### EXPERIMENT ONE

## THE RAINBOW IN A GLASS OF WATER

Fill a glass with water (almost to the top) and place it at the very edge of the countertop in a dark kitchen. Place a sheet of plain white paper on the floor a few inches away from the counter. Put two pieces of masking tape over the front of a flashlight so that the light comes out of a slit about ⅛ inch (0.3 cm) wide. Shine this light across and down into the water as shown in

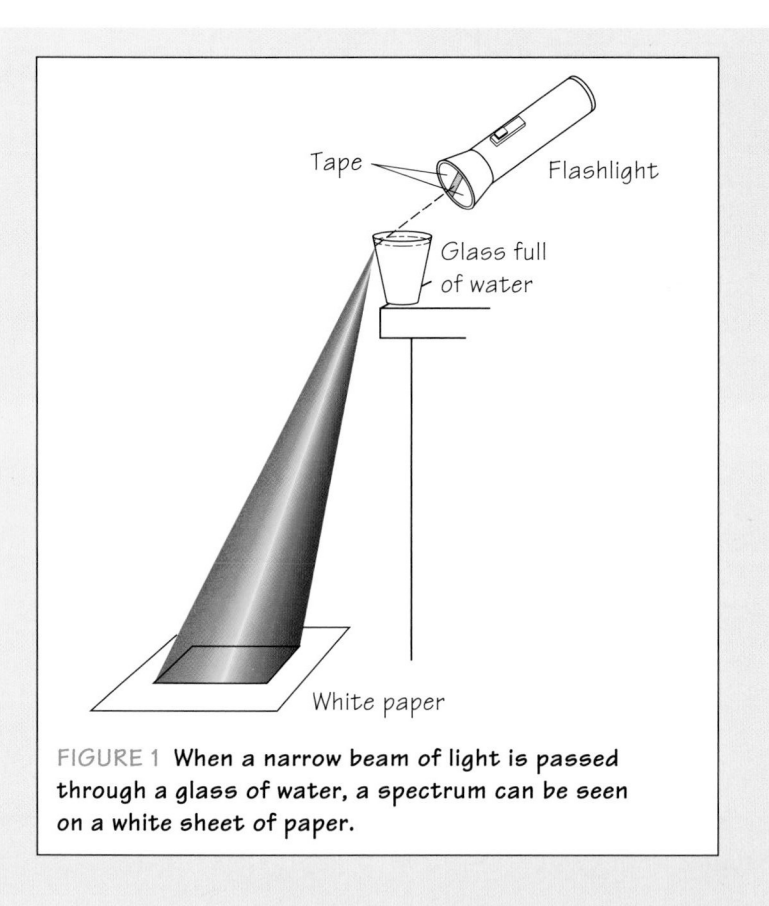

Tape — Flashlight

Glass full of water

White paper

FIGURE 1 **When a narrow beam of light is passed through a glass of water, a spectrum can be seen on a white sheet of paper.**

Figure 1. Can you see a small rainbow on the white paper? If not, move the flashlight around a little until you achieve the best results.

Now that you know what to look for, you will begin to notice small rainbows wherever sunlight falls on water, glass, or plastic that has a tapered shape. Look for rainbows produced by the beveled edge of a mirror or a chandelier.

## NEWTON AND THE SPECTRUM

In 1666, when English scientist Isaac Newton was 24 years old, he saw a rainbow using a triangular glass prism, as shown in Figure 2a. Although many people had done this experiment before Newton, they all believed that the colors came from the prism. Newton was the

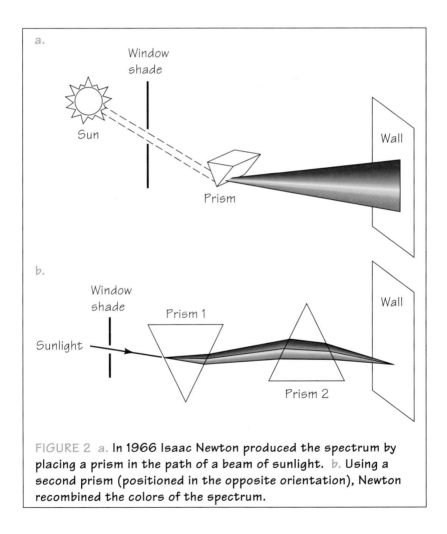

a.

Window shade

Sun

Wall

Prism

b.

Window shade

Prism 1

Wall

Sunlight

Prism 2

FIGURE 2  a. In 1966 Isaac Newton produced the spectrum by placing a prism in the path of a beam of sunlight.  b. Using a second prism (positioned in the opposite orientation), Newton recombined the colors of the spectrum.

first to wonder if the colors were already present in the sunlight and the prism merely separated the colors. By using a second prism to bring the colors together again, he proved that the prism separated the colors. After the light passed through the second spectrum, Newton again saw white light, as shown in Figure 2b.

Newton called the band of colors created by the prism a spectrum. He decided to label the spectrum with just seven colors: red, orange, yellow, green, blue, indigo, and violet. You can remember these seven colors easily—their initials form the name "Roy G. Biv." Newton chose seven colors because the musical scale has seven notes. However, he explained in his writings that there are actually many other colors in the spectrum. (Scientists do not always bother to distinguish indigo in the spectrum, including it as part of the blue colors. That is what we will do in this book.)

## EXPERIMENT TWO

### THE SPECTRUM FROM A PRISM

Place a slide projector on a table about 3 feet (1 m) away from a white wall (or tape white paper on the wall). Cut a 2 inch × 2 inch (5 cm × 5 cm) piece of thin cardboard with a 1-millimeter vertical slot, as shown in Figure 3a. Insert the cardboard "slide" into the slide projector and focus so that there is a sharp vertical line of light on the wall. Place a glass or plastic prism just in front of the lens of the projector and twist the prism so that the "rainbow" is as close to the original line of light as possible—it will still be some distance away.

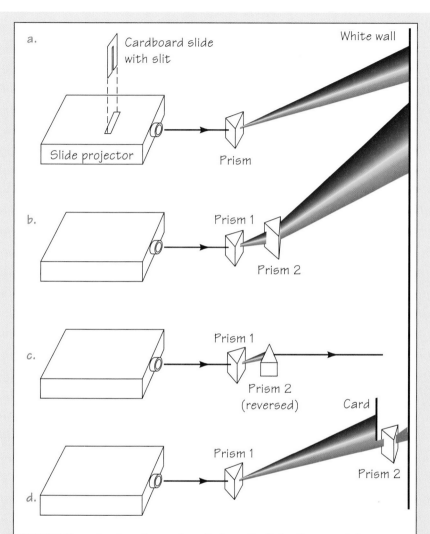

FIGURE 3  a. A prism is produced when the light from a slide projector passes through a prism.  b. If a second prism is added, the spectrum will spread out. No new colors will be produced, however.  c. If a second prism is reversed, the colors of the spectrum will be recombined.  d. If an index card is placed between Prism 1 and the wall and a Prism 2 is placed between the red part of the spectrum and the wall, the red light will spread out.

Now place a second prism just past the first one, exactly as shown in Figure 3b. You will see that, although the spectrum appears farther away and wider, no extra colors show up. Next, reverse the second prism as shown in Figure 3c to recombine the spectrum and get the original white light. (Compare this with Figure 2b.)

Next, remove the second prism. Hold a piece of cardboard about 4 inches (10 cm) from the wall in the path of the spectrum so that only some red shows up on the wall. Place the second prism just behind the card, as shown in Figure 3d. This spreads the red a little more, but notice that no other colors appear. Any narrow part of the spectrum consists of a *monochromatic spectral color*, a color that cannot be split. Because monochromatic spectral colors are not mixtures, they are often called "pure" spectral colors.

Newton's understanding of the spectrum was the beginning of the science of color. He realized that there is no such thing as "colored light." When we look at a red object, the light from it enters our eyes. Our eyes send a message that says "red" to our brain. So colors are really sensations. While it is very convenient to speak of light as if it were colored, we must always remember that it is really not.

Our eyes can see about 10 million different colors. They can see the many colors of the spectrum; they can also see spectral colors mixed with each other, with white, or with black. Mixing colors is a fascinating subject, which you will investigate in Chapter 2.

# REFRACTION

How does a prism make the colors in white light spread out into the spectrum? When a beam of light enters transparent glass, plastic, or water, it usually changes direction—it bends. This is called refraction. Refraction makes it possible for lenses to magnify images.

In a vacuum, light moves at 186,282 miles (299,792 km) per second. In a gas such as air, light slows down a tiny bit. However, when light enters a transparent solid or liquid, it slows down a great deal. Look at Figure 4a. Imagine that aa, bb, cc, dd, ee, ff, and gg represent equal time periods. Since the light beam moves more slowly through the glass, lettered

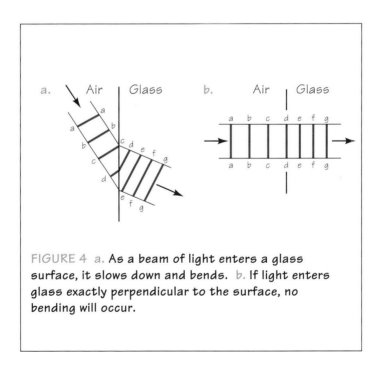

FIGURE 4 a. As a beam of light enters a glass surface, it slows down and bends. b. If light enters glass exactly perpendicular to the surface, no bending will occur.

lines ee, ff, and gg are closer together than aa, bb, and cc. The beam of light slows down because it widens and changes direction when it enters the glass. In other words, the beam of light is refracted.

The only time a beam of light does not bend on entering a substance with a different *refractive index* (RI) is when it enters at a right angle to the surface, as shown in Figure 4b. Some materials bend light more than others. The refractive index tells us how much a material bends light. A perfect vacuum has an RI of 1.0000. Air has an RI of 1.0003; water, 1.33; ordinary glass, 1.50; and diamond, 2.42.

## DISPERSION

The refractive index of a material is a little different for each color of the spectrum. That is why a glass of water or a prism separates the colors in white light. For ordinary glass, the RI for blue light is 1.512, but the RI for red light is 1.498. The difference of 0.014 is called the dispersive refraction or simply the dispersion. Again, some materials have a greater dispersion than others and, therefore, separate the colors more. The dispersion of diamond is 0.044.

## THE RAINBOW

The best-known colors produced by dispersion are seen in the rainbow. Here, sunlight enters one side of a drop of rain and is refracted, creating a spectrum. When the light hits the opposite side of the raindrop, the spectrum is reflected, as shown in Figure 5a. It emerges with the colors still separated by dispersion.

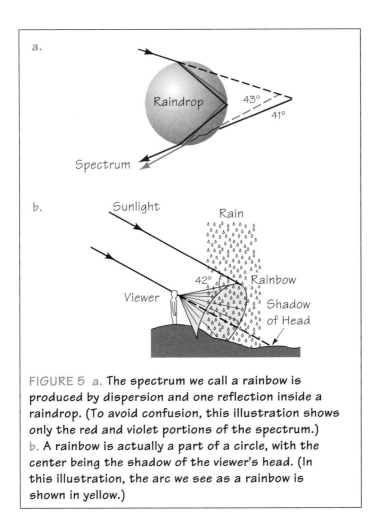

FIGURE 5  a. The spectrum we call a rainbow is produced by dispersion and one reflection inside a raindrop. (To avoid confusion, this illustration shows only the red and violet portions of the spectrum.) b. A rainbow is actually a part of a circle, with the center being the shadow of the viewer's head. (In this illustration, the arc we see as a rainbow is shown in yellow.)

Since this dispersed light comes to us at an angle of about 42 degrees (°), you must have your back to the sun to see the rainbow as an arc, as shown in Figure 5b. You do not need to stand in the rain to see a rainbow, but it must be raining in front of you as you stand with your back to the sun.

## THE GARDEN HOSE RAINBOW

On a sunny day, when the sun is not too high in the sky—before 9:00 A.M. or after 3:00 P.M. is best—stand with your back to the sun. Spray water from a garden hose upward so that the spray falls down through the air in front of you. Adjust the nozzle so that you get a very fine spray lit up by the sun. The rainbow will show up best against something dark, like a hedge or trees. Notice that the rainbow is in the shape of an arc, or part of a circle, and that the shadow of your head is at the center of the circle, as shown in Figure 5b.

A "secondary rainbow" may be seen when there is strong sun, dark sky, and lots of raindrops. Here, there are two *reflections* (instead of one) inside the raindrops, as shown in Figure 6a. The sequence of the colors is reversed in the secondary rainbow, which comes to us at an angle of about 52°, as in Figure 6b. Although additional rainbows (from three or more reflections) can be created in the laboratory, no more than two are ever seen outdoors.

### SUNDOGS AND HALOS

Rainbows are not the only color effects we see in the sky. The small ice crystals often present in cold clouds have prismlike angles that disperse light from the sun. This can create two patches of rainbowlike color, called

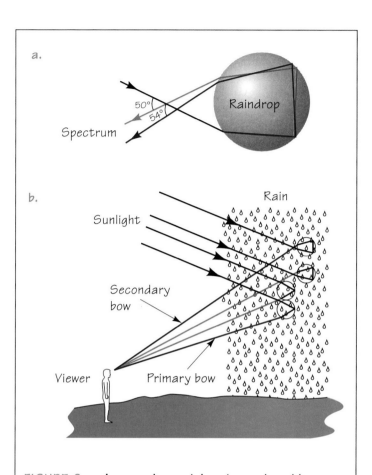

a.

50°
54°
Spectrum
Raindrop

b.

Rain
Sunlight
Secondary bow
Viewer
Primary bow

FIGURE 6  a. A secondary rainbow is produced by dispersion and two reflections inside a raindrop. (To avoid confusion, only red and violet are shown in this illustration.)  b. A secondary rainbow occurs outside the primary rainbow and its color sequence is reverse.

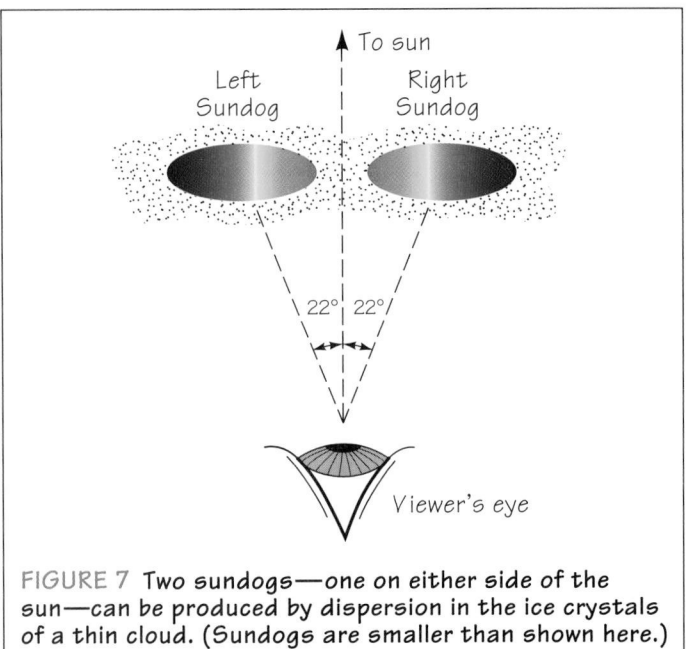

FIGURE 7 Two sundogs—one on either side of the
sun—can be produced by dispersion in the ice crystals
of a thin cloud. (Sundogs are smaller than shown here.)

sundogs. They are called this because they move with
the sun—one in front of it and the other behind it—the
way dogs sometimes walk with people. Sundogs are
seen at an angle of 22° from the sun, as shown in
Figure 7. Look at thin clouds at the same height as the
sun, and well to either side of it. ***Do not look directly
at the sun and always wear dark sunglasses to protect
your eyes and reduce the glare.*** A ring of light or color
called a halo can also come from ice crystals. This
effect is seen occasionally around the sun during the
day, or around the moon at night.

A halo—a colored ring surrounding the sun—can be produced
by ice crystals in a thin cloud.

## THE FIRE IN GEMSTONES

As you read earlier, diamond has a high RI of 2.42 and a very high dispersion of 0.044. The diamonds used in jewelry are designed to make use of these properties. When light falls onto a well-cut diamond, the light is reflected efficiently inside the diamond. As shown in Figure 8, the dispersion gives color called the "fire." Because diamond has a larger RI and a larger dispersion than any other natural gemstone, it shows more flashes of fire than other gems, and sparkles more intensely. You can see the fire for yourself if you look at your mother's engagement ring in a bright light or at diamond rings in the window of a jewelry store.

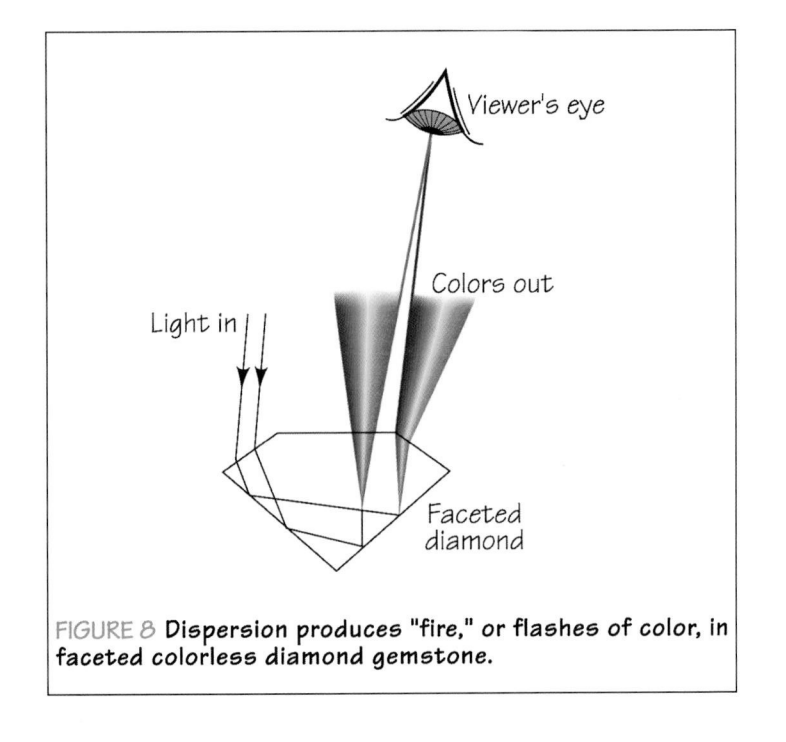

FIGURE 8 **Dispersion produces "fire," or flashes of color, in faceted colorless diamond gemstone.**

# CHAPTER TWO
## COLOR MIXING AND THE COLOR TRIANGLE

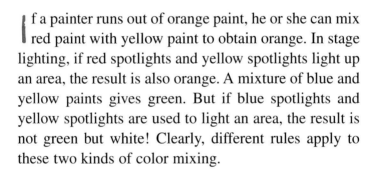

I f a painter runs out of orange paint, he or she can mix red paint with yellow paint to obtain orange. In stage lighting, if red spotlights and yellow spotlights light up an area, the result is also orange. A mixture of blue and yellow paints gives green. But if blue spotlights and yellow spotlights are used to light an area, the result is not green but white! Clearly, different rules apply to these two kinds of color mixing.

### EXPERIMENT FOUR

## MIXING COLORED LIGHTS

For this experiment you need different-colored cellophanes or a set of colored filters (a suitable set of 14 filter slides E-34517 is available from Edmund Scientific, Barrington, NJ, 08007). For best results, use two slide projectors with violet (or blue) and red slides. You will also need a flashlight. Use a rubber band to fasten a green filter and a piece of white tissue paper over the lens. (You could use three flashlights,

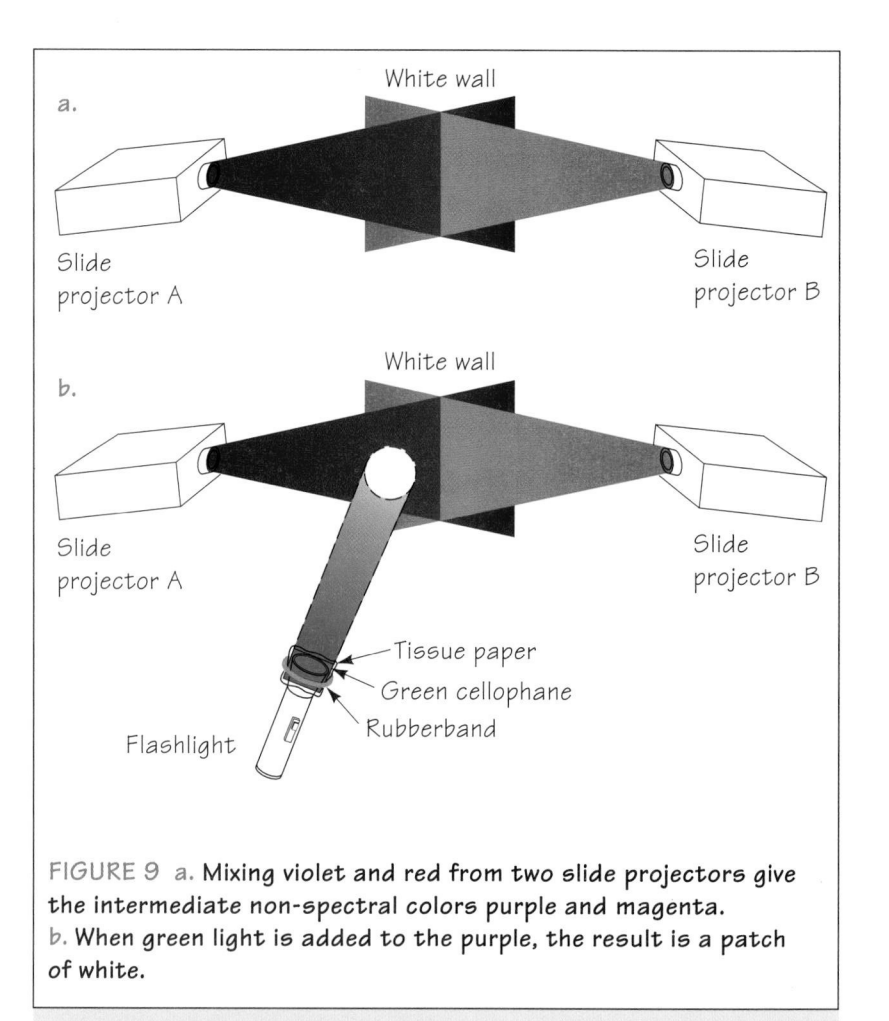

FIGURE 9 a. Mixing violet and red from two slide projectors give the intermediate non-spectral colors purple and magenta.
b. When green light is added to the purple, the result is a patch of white.

but the results will not be as good.) If the cellophane you use is not deeply colored, use several layers.

In a dark room, shine the violet and red lights onto a white wall or white paper so that they overlap, as shown in Figure 9a. You should see the following range of colors: blue close to the violet light source, bluish purple, purple, reddish purple (also called *magenta*), and red close to the red source.

Now shine some green light onto the red area. Adjust the distance until you see yellow. (The green filter is usually not as dark as the red and blue filters, so you have to hold the green source much farther away to balance the colors.)

Next, shine the green light onto the purple region, as shown in Figure 9b. If the distances are just right, you will see white! See if you can obtain white by using slides with different shades of blue and yellow in your two projectors.

## ADDITIVE COLOR MIXING

Mixing colors by combining different colored lights is called *additive color mixing.* The *color triangle,* or *chromaticity diagram,* in Figure 10 includes all the colors our eyes can see at one level of brightness. Notice that Newton's spectral colors, which consist of monochromatic light, follow a U-shaped curve. The colors that fall along the straight line between violet and red are not present in the spectrum.

The colors at the edges of the triangle are strong, or *saturated.* As you move from the saturated yellow at the right of the triangle toward the white region at the center, the yellow becomes mixed with white and looks paler or, *unsaturated.* By looking at Figure 10, you can see that pink is a *nonspectral color.* It is a nonsaturated magenta—a mixture of red, a little blue, and some white.

Every color that can be created by mixing two colored lights falls along a straight line of the color triangle. For example, a dotted line drawn from yel-

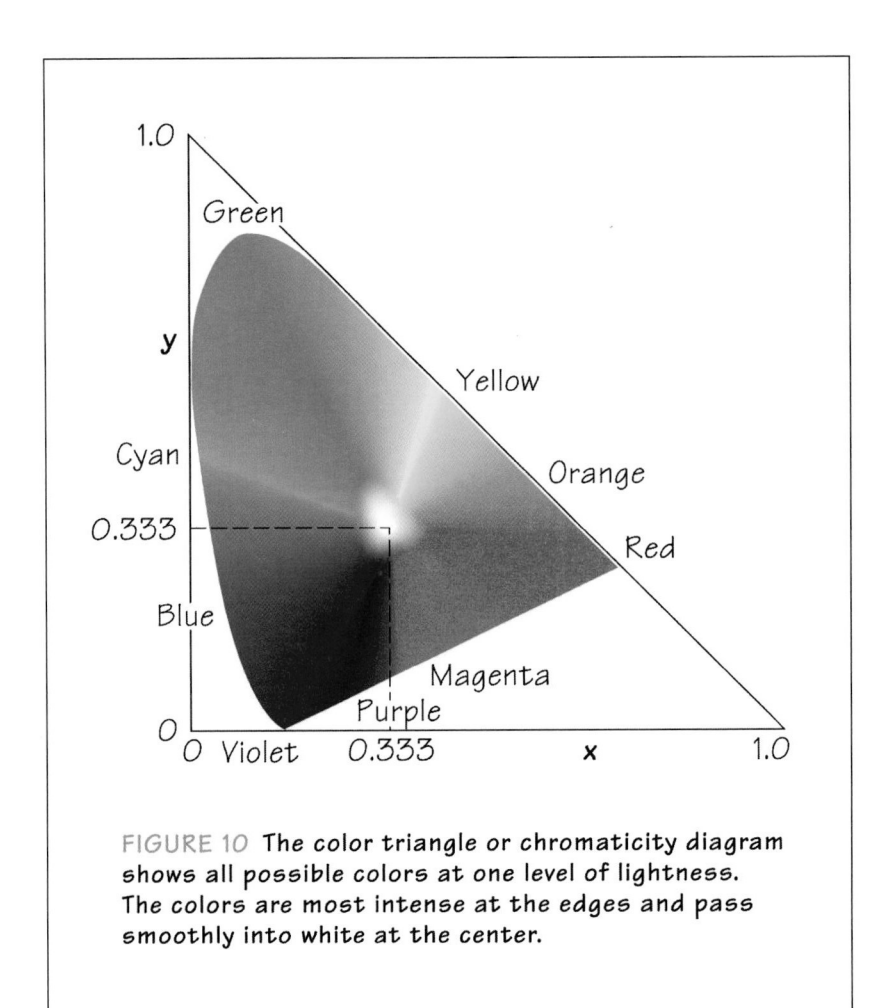

FIGURE 10 **The color triangle or chromaticity diagram
shows all possible colors at one level of lightness.
The colors are most intense at the edges and pass
smoothly into white at the center.**

low to blue on the color triangle in Figure 10 will cross all the colors that can be made by mixing yellow and blue lights, including white. Every color that can be obtained by mixing three colors of light falls inside a triangle made up of lines connecting the three colors within the color triangle.

## COMPLEMENTARY COLORS AND WHITE

We have seen how mixing yellow and blue lights can produce white. White can also be made by mixing any two colors that are on exactly opposite sides of the triangle's central white region. Such pairs of colors are called *complementary colors*. For example, blue and yellow are complementary colors, as are red and *cyan* (a bluish-green color), violet and greenish-yellow, green and purple (or magenta, depending on the exact shade of the green). Try making these and other combinations with your colored light sources.

There are many ways of seeing "white." You can make white by mixing the three colors you used in

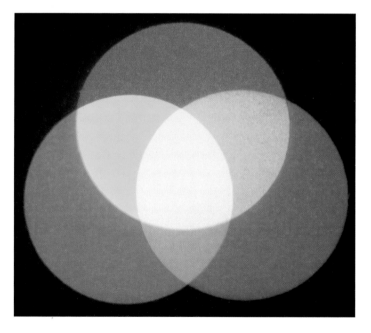

The additive mixing of red, blue, and green light beams gives white.

Experiment 4, by mixing other sets of three colors, or by mixing pairs of complementary colors. There is also the white produced by sunlight, which contains all the spectral colors. The only way to tell which kind of white light you are looking at is to spread it out into the spectrum and see which spectral colors are present.

## COLOR PRINTING AND COLOR TELEVISION

As you now know, by using three colors of light, you can create all the colors that fall within the triangle made by connecting the three colors on the color triangle. If you choose the three colors at the corners of the color triangle—red, violet, and green—you can create all the colors in the whole triangle. This type of additive color mixing is widely used in color printing, stage lighting, and color television.

In color printing, tiny dots of colored inks are printed next to one another. The light reflected from these dots combines by additive color mixing in the eye. Our eyes see only the combined color because the dots are too small to be seen separately. Inks of the three additive primary colors—red, yellow, and violet (or blue)—can be used to produce all colors. However, because this method does not produce dark colors well, extra dots of black ink are added. This is the four-color process used in high-quality color printing. Look at the colors in this book with a magnifying glass.

When the dots overlap, as often happens in the high-speed printing used in newspapers, *subtractive color mixing* occurs. The result may be dull or muddy colors. On a television screen the colors come from either dots or short lines of three colors—green, violet, and red. Use a magnifying glass to look for these colors on a TV screen.

## ACHROMATIC COLORS

Although black is one of the "colors" used in four-color printing, it is not really a color. Black is the absence of all light—what we "see" when our brain receives no light sensations. To speak of a "black color" is an oxymoron (a combination of contradictory words)! The colors in the sequence from white through gray to black are often called *achromatic colors*, or "noncolored colors"—another oxymoron! In the field of color it is, however, appropriate to use both of these descriptions.

## DESCRIBING COLORS

How would you tell someone over the phone that you want paint of a certain color? You could say, "I want a medium shade of bluish green, like green grass but a little more blue and not quite as dark." If you ordered paint this way, chances are that you would not get exactly the color you wanted.

There are, however, several ways to talk about color with precision. You can select any color on Figure 10 by giving the numbers for $x$ and $y$ shown at the edges of the figure—just as you would on a graph or map. White is at $x = 0.333$ and $y = 0.333$, or just (0.333, 0.333). The numbers (0.650, 0.250) describe a red, while (0.500, 0.500) is a yellow. What colors are described by (0.100, 0.700) and (0.100, 0.400)? If you add a third number for the brightness to any such pair of numbers, you can specify any of the 10 million colors we can see.

Another way of describing colors uses a set of three numbers that corresponds to *hue, saturation,* and *light-*

31

*ness*. Hue refers to the colors around the rim of the color triangle. Saturation is greatest at the edges of the triangle, and decreases as white is added. Colors closer to the center of the triangle are less saturated, paler, or weaker variations of the same hue. Lightness is a measure of the amount of light present, transmitted, or reflected. In paint, adding black reduces the lightness.

The human eye can see only one color at one location. In Experiment 4, when you mixed red light and green light, your eye-brain combination gave you the message "yellow." Your brain will receive exactly the same message if you see spectral yellow light in the spectrum. This is how our eyes work. Different mixtures that look the same to the eye are called *metamers* or *metameric mixtures*. With paints or dyes, metamers may look the same in one kind of light, such as daylight, but may have a different color under another kind of light, such as indoor lighting.

## SUBTRACTIVE COLOR MIXING

In subtractive color mixing, some of the colors are subtracted—or removed—from white light. In Experiment 4, the colored cellophane you placed in the slide projectors or over flashlights made colored light by subtracting some components of white light from the mixture.

If you take some of the colors away from ordinary white light containing the full spectrum, how can you tell what color is left? The answer is that you will see the color that is complementary to what was taken away. For example, if you remove yellow from white, you get blue. If you remove blue from white, you get yellow. If you remove red from white, you get cyan. And so on.

The subtractive mixing when light passes through filters of magenta, cyan, and yellow gives black.

## COLOR FILTERS

Use the arrangement shown in Figure 3a to obtain a spectrum. Place a red filter or cellophane between the lens and the prism. Notice that this filter lets red, orange, and perhaps a little yellow pass through it, but absorbs all the other colors of the spectrum. This is how the filter works to transmit light of a color that your eye sees as red. The transmitted color is a mixture, but it has exactly the same effect on the eye as a spectral color near the middle of the transmitted range of spectral colors.

Now remove the red filter and replace it with a violet (or a dark-blue) one. Notice that this filter lets violet, blue, and perhaps a little green pass through it, but absorbs all the other colors of the spectrum. Now put the red filter on top of the violet one. No color can get through this combination because all the colors of the spectrum are absorbed by either one filter or the other. Recall that with additive color mixing, red and violet together give a purple color, but here, with subtractive mixing, red and violet give the achromatic color black.

Paints contain fine powders called *pigments* that give them color. Red pigment gives a deep-red paint by removing or "absorbing" all light other than red. The pigment then reflects or transmits only red light. In a medium-intensity red paint, the pigment reflects or transmits not only red but also orange and some yellow, just as a color filter does. The result is an unsaturated red color.

## EXPERIMENT SIX

## MIXING PAINTS

You will need some deep-red, deep-green, and deep-blue oil or latex paints. (Watercolors do not work as well in these experiments because they do not give saturated colors.) Mix together a little of each of these three paints. The pigment in the deep-blue paint absorbs all colored light except blue and a little green and violet.

But these colors are absorbed by the pigments in the other two paints. All colors should be absorbed by the mixture and no light should remain, which would then leave black.

If you try this experiment, you will probably get a dark gray rather than a full black because the absorptions will not be complete if the paints are not fully saturated. Paint that is really black is made by using a special black pigment that absorbs all the colors completely. Remember that in Experiment 4, which involved additive color mixing, red, green, and blue (or violet) gave you white, the opposite of the black obtained in subtractive mixing!

Now mix some red and blue paints and you will see that you get purple or magenta. This subtractive color mixture gives the same results as the additive color mixing for these two colors. Next combine some yellow paint with blue paint. You get green from this subtractive color mixing instead of the white produced with additive mixing of these same colors in Experiment 4! Try other subtractive color mixtures and think about the results.

Any color paint can be made in many different ways. Orange paint can be made by using a single orange pigment or a metameric mixture of pigments, such as red and yellow. That explains why mixing paints that appear to be the same color can give you slightly different results.

You can obtain additional nonspectral colors in subtractive color mixing, such as brown (a mixture of orange and black) and olive (a mixture of yellowish green and black). Subtractive color mixing is also used in *dyes*. A dye is a colored liquid used to give color to cloth, paper, leather, and so on. Dyes also give color to the inks used in pens and markers. Green dyes are often mixtures of a yellow dye and a blue dye. Black dyes usually consist of a mixture of strongly absorbing dyes of several colors that absorb the whole spectrum.

## COLOR AND SURFACES

Curious things happen when a colored substance is ground up to make a pigment for use in a paint. Transparent colorless glass is a good example. It does not absorb light, but it transmits light very well because the light is not scattered.

However, if you grind this glass into a fine powder, the powder will neither absorb nor transmit light. Light falling on the powder is scattered in all directions by reflections from the many surfaces on the powder particles. Since there is no absorption, there is no change in the color when it is ground. As a result, the powder looks white.

Next, consider a transparent substance, such as glass, that is colored because it absorbs some colors. We see it as colored because the light that is not absorbed is transmitted through it. Again, there is no scattering. If you grind this colored substance into a coarse powder, with particles measuring about 4/1,000 inch (1/100 mm), light will be absorbed inside each powder particle. The colored light that is not absorbed is scattered in all directions by reflections from the many particle surfaces. The same thing happens in the pigment in a paint.

What happens if you grind the powder too fine, perhaps 100 times smaller? There will now be so many reflections from the particle surfaces that very little light can enter the particles and be absorbed. As a result, the pigment will look very pale or even white.

When the surface of a colored substance is smooth, like highly polished metal or glossy paint, you will see little of its color if you are positioned at an angle where light is strongly reflected from its surface. Look at a color figure in this book from different angles to see this effect. If the surface of a colored object is rough, it can act in either of two ways. It may act like a coarse powder. If this is the case, you will be able to see the color when there is no strong surface reflection. Alternatively, it may act like a very fine powder and hide the color.

## PRIMARY COLORS

A few colors can be used in mixtures to obtain a wide range of colors. These colors are often called primary colors. When you look at color printing or a color television screen, you usually see colors created by mixing red, green, and blue (or violet). These three colors, which can be found at the corners of the color triangle in Figure 10, are called *additive primary colors*.

Artists and other people who mix paints, pigments, or dyes usually use red, yellow, and blue. These are the *subtractive primary colors*. However, their "red" is usually a magenta and their "blue" is usually a cyan. Think about it, and you will see that it is not a coincidence that the three subtractive primary colors are complementary to the three additive primary colors.

Artists usually use more than just the primary colors

in their paintings—for a very good reason. Think about mixing a yellow paint with a blue paint to obtain green. The yellow paint will absorb some green light and so will the blue paint. While the mixture does produce a green, it will be an unsaturated green because both paints absorb some green from white light. A paint made from a pure deep-green pigment may absorb no green at all and will therefore give a more saturated green than the mixture.

Another set of primary colors consists of four colors. This set is often used in studies of the eye and vision, using the complementary primary colors yellow, "red" (actually a magenta), "blue" (on the violet side), and "green" (on the cyan side).

To understand the mixing of colors more completely, you need to explore the nature of light and color as well as the way we see color.

# CHAPTER THREE
## LIGHT, COLOR, ELECTRONS, AND THE EYE

### THE NATURE OF LIGHT

Starting with the ancient Greeks, some people believed that light consists of tiny particles that hit our eyes. Other people thought that light exists as a wave, just as sound does. We now know that both groups were right! Some experiments show that light is made up of particles—and not waves; others indicate that light consists of waves—and not particles! For a long time these results confused scientists.

The final understanding of this problem came from *quantum theory*. According to quantum theory, light usually behaves like tiny particles called *photons*, but a photon can also act as if it consisted of a wave. One photon is the smallest amount of any spectral color light that can exist by itself. This amount is also the same as the smallest packet of same-color light waves that can exist by itself. This must be so because the photon and the wave are exactly the same.

Sometimes it is convenient to talk about light as consisting of waves, while at other times we talk about it as consisting of particles. A sound wave needs air to carry it. Sound waves compress the air they pass through and we hear the sound when the compression hits our ears. A water wave needs water to carry it. But a light wave (or photon) does not need a material to carry it. Light can pass through a vacuum as well as through transparent materials such as glass, water, and plastic.

Light is a form of energy. In everyday activities, energy cannot be created or destroyed, but it can be changed from one form of energy to another. Therefore, if you wish to produce light, you must provide energy. The energy in a flame's light comes from the chemical energy of burning. The energy in the light emitted by a lightbulb comes from electricity. When light is absorbed, the photon of light disappears but its energy has to go somewhere. This energy can show itself as warmth on our skin or as an electrical message that travels from our eye to our brain. The visible spectrum that we call light ends at red and at violet, but there is also energy beyond both these colors.

## THE ELECTROMAGNETIC SPECTRUM

Newton's spectrum is part of the much larger *electromagnetic spectrum* shown in Figure 11a. It is called "electromagnetic" because the spectrum has both electric and magnetic properties. It also has many different forms of energy. Beyond the red end of the visible spectrum is *infrared (IR)*, or radiant heat, which we can feel on our skin but cannot see with our eyes. Beyond infrared are the microwaves we use to heat food and the radio waves that bring us radio and television.

Beyond the violet end of the visible spectrum there

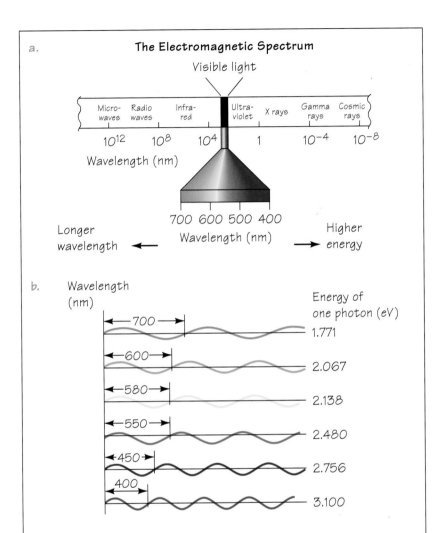

FIGURE 11 a. The electromagnetic spectrum is composed of electromagnetic radiation over a broad range of wavelengths. The visible spectrum is only a small portion of the electromagntic spectrum. b. The wavelengths in nanometers of the visible spectrum ranges from 700 nm for red to 400 nm for violet. The energy per photon in electron volts ranges from 1.771 eV for red to 3.100 eV for violet.

is *ultraviolet (UV)*, which gives us our tans and sunburns. We cannot see ultraviolet but it can damage our eyes. Beyond ultraviolet are X rays, which are used to study the inside of our bodies, as well as gamma rays and cosmic rays.

A position along the electromagnetic spectrum can be identified in several ways. Take the monochromatic spectral yellow light called "sodium yellow," for example. You can express the energy of a photon of this light in units of *electron volts (eV)*. One eV is the energy acquired by a free electron when it speeds up due to a potential difference of 1 volt. The energy of sodium yellow light is 2.10 eV.

Instead of giving the energy of the photon, you could express this quantity in *wavelengths*. Sodium yellow—yellow of energy 2.10 eV—has a wavelength

## TABLE 1 WAVELENGTH AND ENERGY OF COLORS IN THE VISIBLE SPECTRUM

| COLOR | WAVELENGTH | ENERGY |
|---|---|---|
| Red | 700 nm* | 1.771 eV |
| Reddish orange | 650 nm | 1.909 eV |
| Orange | 600 nm | 2.067 eV |
| Yellow | 580 nm | 2.138 eV |
| Yellowish green | 550 nm | 2.254 eV |
| Green | 500 nm | 2.480 eV |
| Blue | 450 nm | 2.756 eV |
| Violet | 400 nm* | 3.100 eV |

* Approximate limit of our color vision

of 589 *nanometers*. A nanometer (nm) is 1 billionth or $10^{-9}$ of a meter. Just as inches can easily be converted to centimeters, energy in electron volts can be converted to wavelength in nanometers as follows:

(energy in eV) = 1240/(wavelength in nm)

(wavelength in nm) = 1240/(energy in eV).

## MEASURING THE VISIBLE SPECTRUM

Typical values for some colors of the spectrum are given in Table 1 and Figure 11b. Note that the wavelength gets smaller as the energy gets larger.

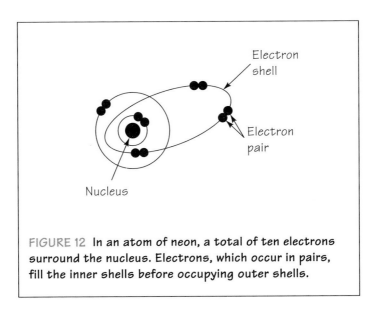

FIGURE 12 **In an atom of neon, a total of ten electrons surround the nucleus. Electrons, which occur in pairs, fill the inner shells before occupying outer shells.**

## ELECTRONS AND LIGHT

An atom is the smallest part of an element that has the properties of that element. Each atom consists of a nucleus surrounded by one or more *electrons*. See Figure 12. Electrons are so small that it takes more than 1 billion billion billion ($10^{27}$) electrons to weigh 1 gram. Yet, tiny as they are, we can see individual electrons at work when we see light or color.

The number of electrons surrounding the nucleus of an atom increases from 1 for hydrogen to more than 100 for the heaviest atoms we know. The electrons in each atom are arranged in groups called *electron shells*. Each shell can hold a certain number of electrons. When a shell in an atom is full, all the electrons in that shell are paired. Atoms like to reach an arrangement where all the electrons are paired up. See Figure 12.

All matter—whether solid, liquid, or gas—is made up of atoms or *molecules*. Most of the time, atoms combine to form molecules in one of two ways. An atom can give one or more electrons to another atom so that both atoms have full shells and all electrons are paired up. Or atoms can share some electrons with each other in pairs so that, again, all electrons are paired up. We learn about these arrangements in the study of chemistry.

There are no atoms present in a vacuum so light can travel freely at its usual speed. When light enters matter, it interacts or "visits" briefly with the electrons on the first atom or molecule it encounters. Then, it passes on to "visit" the electrons of the next atom or molecule in its path, and so on. This process causes light to slow down. In air, which has only 24 billion billion molecules per cubic centimeter, light slows down only a little bit. In water, which has 1,200 times more molecules per cubic centimeter than air, light slows down to three-quarters of the speed it achieves in a vacuum. In solids with a high refractive index, such as diamond, light slows down to less than one-half of its speed in a vacuum. The speed is given by 100/RI percent of the speed in a vacuum.

As you saw earlier in this chapter, photons of different color light have different wavelengths and energies. Violet has a shorter wavelength and a higher energy than any other color, so it interacts more strongly with electrons. Therefore, when passing through matter, violet slows down more than any other color.

This slowing down produces the refractive index differences you observed when you placed a prism in the path of a light beam. It also explains how electrons in atoms and molecules produce the dispersion you learned about in Chapter 1. It even explains why the violet end of the spectrum—with higher-energy photons—is deflected more than other colors and why red, with lower-energy photons, is deflected least. Take another look at Figures 2 and 3.

## THE EYE AND COLOR VISION

The eye is a ball filled with a transparent liquid, as shown in Figure 13 on the next page. It has a lens, which uses refraction to focus the light that enters the eye onto the retina at the back of the eyeball. The retina, a thin layer of tissue that is sensitive to light, contains a network of nerve cells. The optic nerve carries information from the nerve cells in the retina to the brain. The iris is the colored part of the eye. At the center of the iris is a round opening called the pupil. It opens up in dim light and closes down in bright light to adjust the amount of light entering the eye.

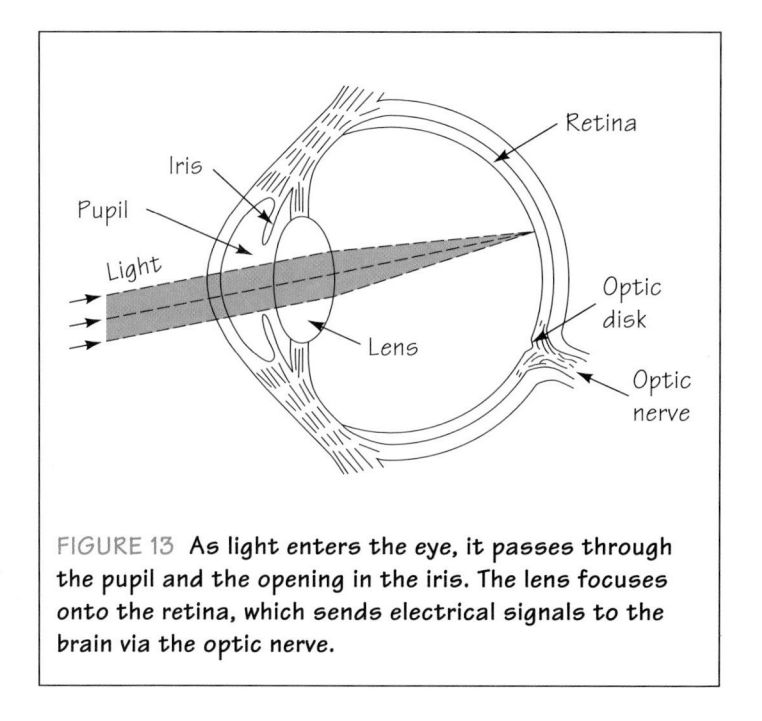

FIGURE 13 As light enters the eye, it passes through
the pupil and the opening in the iris. The lens focuses
onto the retina, which sends electrical signals to the
brain via the optic nerve.

The retina is lined with tiny cells called rods, which
are extremely sensitive to light. They let us see in very
dim light, but without any color, as mentioned in the
introduction. There are also three types of tiny cones on
the surface of the retina. They give us color vision in
brighter light. There are more than 100 million rods
and cones in each eye.

If you have trouble seeing the color effects described
in this book, you may have a color vision defect, sometimes called color blindness. About 1 in 20 males and
about 1 in 200 females has some type of color vision deficiency. Some such people find it difficult or impossible to
distinguish reds from greens. The total inability to see
any colors at all is extremely rare. An ophthalmologist
(eye specialist) can easily test for color deficiency.

# THE BLIND SPOT

There are no rods or cones in the optic disk (Figure 13)—the spot where the optic nerve exits the eyeball. This means that each of our eyes has a blind spot. Cover your left eye and look with your right eye at the square in Figure 14, held at arm's length. Notice that you are aware that the circle is there even though you are looking at the square. Now move the page slowly toward you. Keep looking at the square and notice that the circle suddenly disappears at a certain distance. Now cover your right eye and look at the circle. What happens to the square?

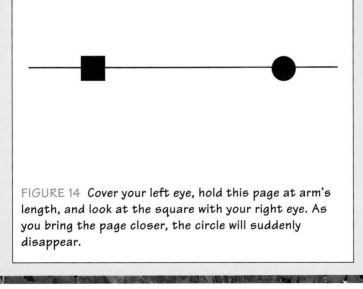

FIGURE 14 Cover your left eye, hold this page at arm's length, and look at the square with your right eye. As you bring the page closer, the circle will suddenly disappear.

Some night-active animals, such as owls, have only rods in their eyes. Although these animals cannot see color, they have excellent night vision. Some animals have rods and cones that work differently than ours. For example, the colors seen by bees go beyond the violet end of the spectrum. Bees do not see red, but they do see orange, yellow, green, blue, violet, and even some ultraviolet.

## EXPERIMENT EIGHT

## SEEING COLORS

Our eyes can be tricked by the conditions under which we look at colors:

- Cut out two 4-inch (10-cm) squares from a sheet of green paper and place one of the squares on a sheet of blue paper and the other on a sheet of yellow, orange, or red paper. The two green squares now look different in color. If you don't see the difference, ask someone to compare the colors—someone who does not know that the two green squares were cut from the same sheet of paper. Try this experiment using other colors. The effect you are observing is called simultaneous color contrast.

- In a dark room, shine a flashlight onto a large sheet of white paper or a white wall to make a small spot of white light. Notice its color. Now cover another flashlight with yellow cellophane. By holding it farther away from the white paper, form a much larger area of pale-yellow light around the small spot made by the first flashlight. You will see that the small spot now looks bluish, which is the color complementary to yellow. This effect is also the result of simultaneous color contrast. Try this experiment using other colors.

- Stare at the upper black dot in Figure 15 on the next page and count slowly to ten; you can blink but do not move your head or your eyes. Now quickly stare at the lower black dot. Since the color system in your eyes is a little tired from the first staring, you will begin to see the colors that are complementary to yellow and green! These colors are called afterimages, and this effect is called successive color contrast.

- In a dark room, light a candle and cast the shadow of a pencil onto a white surface. Notice that the shadow is dark and has no color. Now shine a flashlight on the white surface to light up the shadow and the area around it. The shadow will have a bluish color. Blue is the complementary color of the yellow in the candle flame. This effect is called colored shadows.

- Sometimes we "see" colors that are not really there. In a dark room, close your eyes and gently press your hands against them. This excites the optic nerves and produces color. A hard knock on the head can make us see colored "stars." (Do not try this!)

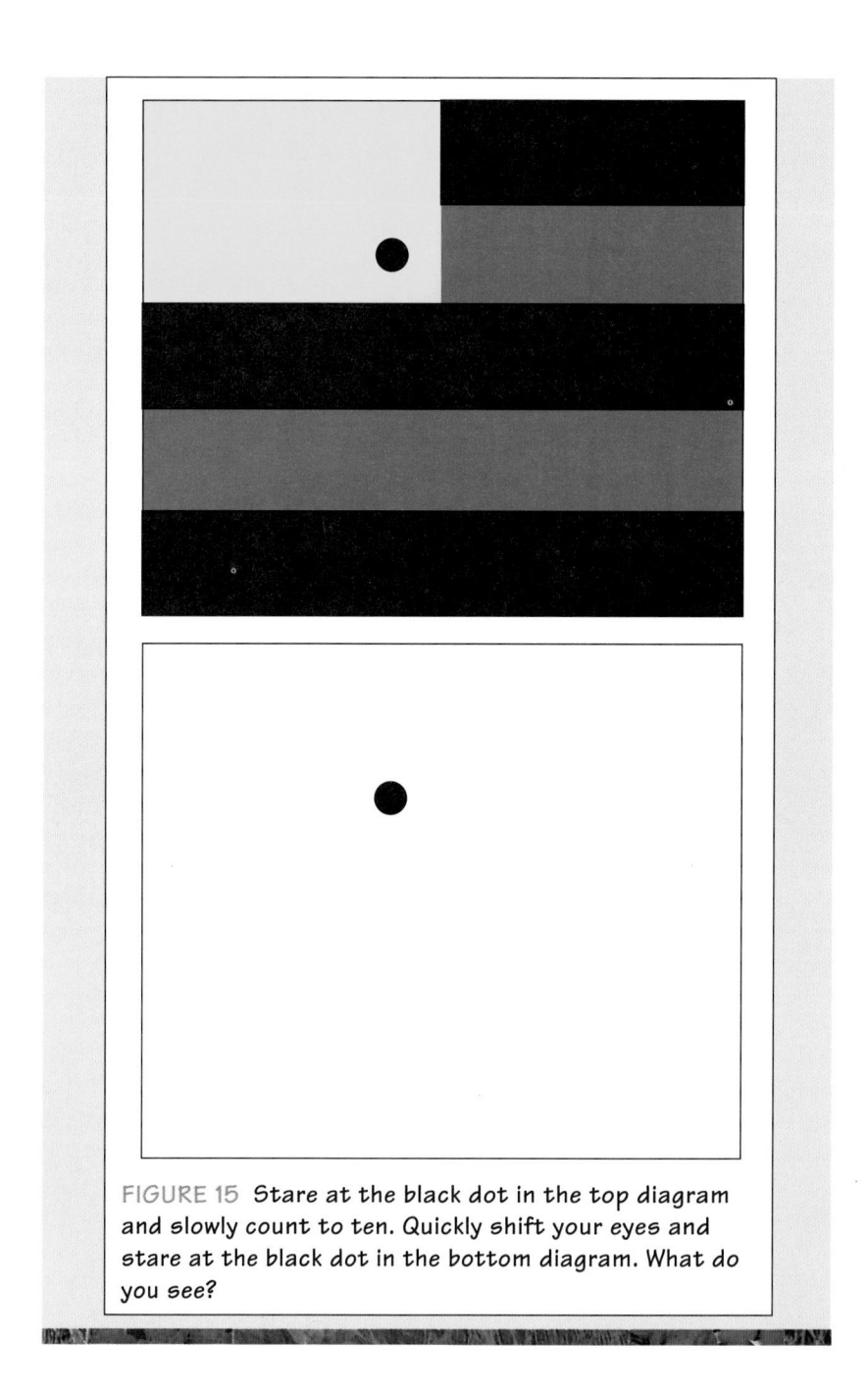

FIGURE 15 Stare at the black dot in the top diagram and slowly count to ten. Quickly shift your eyes and stare at the black dot in the bottom diagram. What do you see?

# CHAPTER FOUR
## BLUE SKY, BLUE EYES, RED SUNSET

Have you ever wondered what causes the blue color of a clear sky, the color in blue eyes, or the bluish skin of a light-colored person who is feeling cold? And why is the sky filled with beautiful orange and red colors when the sun is setting? All these colors are produced by a single phenomenon—*scattering*.

### EXPERIMENT NINE

### RED SUNSET AND BLUE SKY IN A GLASS

You will need two glasses that are half full of water. Stir a few drops of milk into one of the glasses. In a dark room, shine a flashlight through the diluted milk, as shown in Figure 16 on the next page. Let the light fall onto a sheet of white paper or look into the light that has passed through the milk. Now do the same with the other glass. The light passing through the diluted milk is reddish compared to the light passing through the glass that contains only water. Next, return to the glass containing the milk and look at it

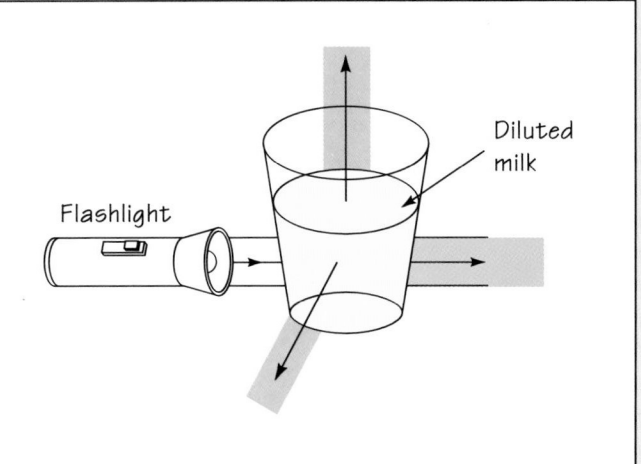

FIGURE 16 **The particles in water containing a little milk scatter light from the flashlight. The light that has passed through the milk should look reddish. If you look at the glass from the top or side, the light should look bluish.**

from the side or the top. You will notice that the beam of light passing through the milk looks bluish. Adding a little more milk may give you more obvious results.

## BLUE SKY AND RED SUNSET

The blue of a clear sky and the red of a sunrise or sunset are created in the same way as the colors you saw in Experiment 9. White light from the sun passes through the air above us, as shown in Figure 17. The violet, blue, and green parts of the white light are scattered in all directions by dust and molecules in the air in Figure 17 as they are by tiny fat particles in the milk in

Experiment 9. We see this scattered mixture of colors as blue.

The sun looks yellowish white at noon because only a little of the violet, blue, and green light is missing. ***Be careful! Looking at the sun can damage your eyes. Use very dark or double sunglasses.*** At sunset or sunrise, there is more air between us and the sun,  so that almost all of the violet, blue, and green is missing. Only the yellow, orange, and red colors of light are left. That is why we see an orange to deep-red color. From space or from the moon, the sky always looks black and the sun always looks white because there is no air and, therefore, no scattering.

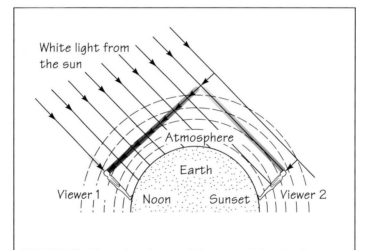

FIGURE 17 **Air molecules and dust particles in the air scatter sunlight so that the sky looks blue. Scattering also causes the sun to look yellow at noon and red just before dusk.**

Sunsets are more spectacular than sunrises because damp soil dries up during the heat of the day and turns into dust. The dust is stirred up into the air by the activities of people, animals, and the wind. The result is stronger scattering. The most beautiful sunsets occur when a volcano throws large amounts of volcanic ash high into the upper atmosphere. This dust can remain in the atmosphere for months or even years.

Smog, the result of air pollution caused by human activity, also makes the scattering stronger. Trees in forests and jungles produce their own pollution, causing "summer heat haze" or "natural smog." The Blue Ridge Mountains are named for this effect. Although you may not realize it, you take this scattering into account when you estimate the distance to faraway mountains. You can be fooled when rain washes the air clean of dust. The mountains seem to be closer because scattering is reduced.

## SCATTERING

Scattering is caused by electrons in molecules and in particles that are smaller than the wavelength of the light; that is, smaller than about 400 nanometers (nm). (It would take a row of 25,000 such particles to make 1 centimeter.) While scattering occurs at all wavelengths, it is much stronger at shorter wavelengths (the violet end of the spectrum).

If you are mathematically inclined, you may wish to know that the intensity of scattering is inversely proportional to the fourth power of the wavelength $w$; that is, proportional to $w^{-4}$. This means that violet at 400 nm is scattered $(700/400)^4 = 9.4$ times more than red at 700 nm. Scattering is strongest at the violet end of the spectrum because the light there has more energy to interact with electrons. Remember, from the refraction discussion in Chapter 3, that higher-energy light is also bent the most.

Blue colors created by scattering can be seen in many unexpected places. The color of blue eyes is caused by the scattering of fine particles of fat and protein in the iris. It is seen against dark pigments at the back of the iris. If there is also a yellow pigment in the front of the iris, it combines subtractively with the bluish white of the scattering to give a green color. With more and darker pigments in the front of the iris, the blue cannot be seen. The result is brown or black eyes. In albinos, all pigments are missing. The blue from the scattering combines additively with white reflections from the back of the eye and red reflections from its blood vessels to produce pink.

In a similar way, the weak blue from scattering in a light-colored skin combines additively with white reflection and red from blood vessels just below the surface of the skin to give a pink color. When this type of skin is cold, blood vessels in the surface of the skin shrink to save heat and we see the bluish-white skin color by itself. When this skin is hot, the blood vessels expand so that the blood can carry away the heat and the skin turns red. The same thing happens with the flush of embarrassment. In animals, most blue colors come from scattering, including the blue on the bare skin patches of monkeys, on the feathers of birds, on the wings of butterflies, and on jellyfish. These blue colors are often combined with yellow pigments to produce the green color on birds, chameleons, snakes, and lizards.

The pink eyes of albinos are colored by a combination of pale blue from scattering and pale red from blood vessels.

## SCATTERING IN A BLUE FEATHER

Look for a blue feather, such as a feather from a blue jay. Soak a blue piece of the feather for a few hours in a glass containing some rubbing alcohol (70 percent isopropyl alcohol). Because alcohol has about the same refractive index as the feather, scattering will be reduced and you will be able to see the black backing, which made the blue color saturated. If you take the feather out of the alcohol and let it dry for a few minutes, the blue color will return.

Now, place the feather on a hard surface and *carefully* hit part of a blue region firmly with a hammer, but don't hit it hard enough to destroy it totally. The crushing breaks up the structure that causes the scattering. Again, you can see the black backing, but this time you cannot get the blue back.

The blues of scattering are saturated, or deeply colored, only when there is a black background. The black of outer space provides the backing for the blue of the sky.

When the scattering particles are much larger than the wavelength of light, all wavelengths are scattered equally and the scattered light remains white. This happens with fog, steam, mist, and most clouds.

# CHAPTER FIVE

## SOAP BUBBLES, OIL SLICKS, CDS, AND OPALS

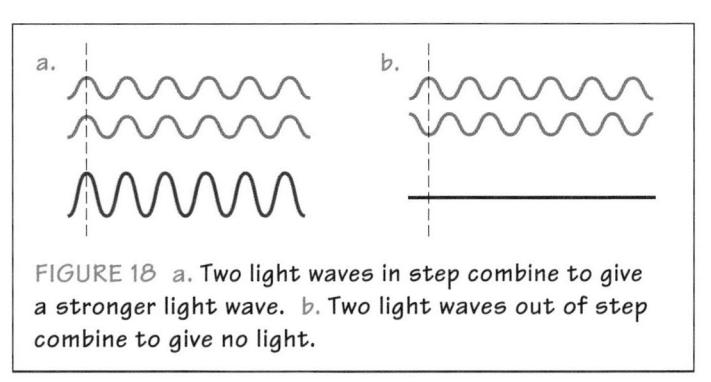

H ave you ever watched the brilliant colors of a soap bubble floating through the air in bright sunlight? These colors are the result of *interference*. A special kind of interference called *diffraction* gives color to CDs (compact disks) and the gemstone opal.

FIGURE 18  a. Two light waves in step combine to give a stronger light wave.  b. Two light waves out of step combine to give no light.

### WAVES IN AND OUT OF STEP

A curious thing happens when two waves of the same wavelength move side by side. If the waves are in step, they combine. The result is a single wave that is twice as strong as the two separate waves. See Figure 18.

However, if the waves are out of step, the two waves cancel each other out. This is true of all kinds of waves: sound waves, the ripples on water, and light waves. Because the two waves interfere with each other, this effect is called interference. When two waves destroy each other, their energy appears at a spot where other waves are combining. The total energy in the system remains the same.

Now think of a monochromatic beam of light, as at *AB* in Figure 19, falling on a thin film of transparent material such as the film of a bubble. One part of the beam is reflected at *C* on the upper surface of the film. This reflected beam moves in direction *D*. Another part of the beam enters the film and is then reflected at *E* on the lower surface of the film. This beam also moves in

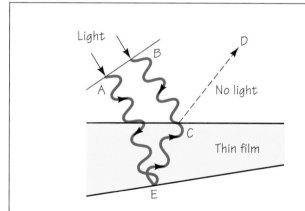

FIGURE 19 **When light wave** *AB* **enters a thin film, part of the beam is reflected at** *C* **and moves in direction** *D*. **Another part of the beam is reflected at** *E* **and moves in direction** *D*. **If the beams of light at** *D* **are out of step, they combine and cancel each other out.**

direction *D*. If the two beams of light are out of step, then they cancel each other out. The result, is no light.

If the soap-bubble film is just a little thinner, then the two beams might combine to make extra strong light. With an even thinner film, they again cancel each other out. So when light of a single color falls on a thin, tapered film, we see alternating stripes of strong light and no light. When white light falls on such a film, this same process happens separately for each spectral color.

As explained by Newton the exact color at any spot depends only on the thickness of the film and on the refractive index of the film material. The very thinnest films are black—they show no light reflection at all. Table 2 lists the colors you will see if you look at soap-

## TABLE 2 THE COLOR OF SOAP BUBBLES

| THICKNESS (nm) | COLOR | THICKNESS (nm) | COLOR |
|---|---|---|---|
| 20 (or less) | Black | 350 | Yellow |
| 25 | Gray | 370 | Orange-red |
| 60 | Gray-blue | 410 | Violet |
| 100 | White | 430 | Blue |
| 120 | Yellow | 510 | Green |
| 160 | Yellow-brown | 550 | Yellow |
| 190 | Orange-red | 580 | Red-violet |
| 200 | Red | 700 | Green |
| 220 | Violet | 800 | Pink |
| 260 | Blue | 900 | Green |
| 280 | Green | 1000 | Pink |

The colors seen in soap bubbles are produced by interference. (The actual colors are iridescent, or metallic-like, but this effect cannot be reproduced in print.)

bubble films of various thicknesses. Films that are thicker than 1,000 nm continue to alternate between green and pink, but the colors rapidly get weaker.

## IRIDESCENT INTERFERENCE COLORS

The reflection produced by interference is brilliant and looks metallic in bright light. It is often called *iridescence*. We find iridescence surprising because we usually see such brilliant reflections only on mirrors and polished metal.

# IRIDESCENT INTERFERENCE COLORS

Do this experiment on a bright sunny day. You will need a container of soap-bubble solution with a plastic loop. Alternatively, you could make a wire loop about 1 inch (2.5 cm) across and use dishwashing liquid mixed with a little bit of water. Dip the loop into the soap solution and, with your back to the sun, hold the film in the loop upright. Notice the brilliant iridescent colors in the film.

As the soap solution drains downward, the upper part of the film gets thinner and turns black. Using Table 2 on page 60, you can determine the thickness of the different parts of your film. To give you an idea of these sizes, the 200-nm film that gives red is only 1/50,000 cm thick.

Use a garden hose or a watering can to make a small puddle on a black top driveway or on dark soil. Add a few drops of cooking oil, one drop at a time, and watch the color of the water change as the oil spreads. These iridescent colors will be strongest when the sun is shining. After a rainstorm, you can often see these oil-slick colors at a gas station.

In addition to soap bubbles and oil slicks, you can also see iridescent interference colors on the transparent wings of houseflies and dragonflies. You need bright sunlight to see iridescence from a single film. Interference colors change when we look at them from different angles.

## MULTILAYER INTERFERENCE

In nature and in technology, several films stacked on top of each other give especially brilliant iridescent colors. These multiple-layer interference films show strong iridescence even on a dull day or in ordinary indoor lighting.

If you look at the lens on a high-quality camera or pair of binoculars, you will see iridescent colors. The surface of clean glass reflects about one-twentieth of the light falling onto it, thus reducing the clarity of the transmitted image. These lenses have been given an antireflection coating, which prevents most reflections, but some multiple-layer interference colors can still be seen.

You can see many brilliant multilayer interference colors in nature. Look at the feathers of a peacock, parrot, or hummingbird; the scales of most fish; and the skins of many snakes. Multilayer interference is also responsible for the metallic-like coloring of many butterflies and beetles. Many night-active animals have excellent night vision due to a multiple-layer interference film at the back of their eyeballs. When you are traveling at night, notice the metallic-like iridescent reflection from the eyes of roadside animals lit up by your headlights.

## DIFFRACTION

Interference can also produce color in the process called diffraction. When any kind of wave—light, sound, or water—passes by the edge of an object, it spreads a little around and behind the object. Look at the waves passing by a rock in Figure 20 on the next

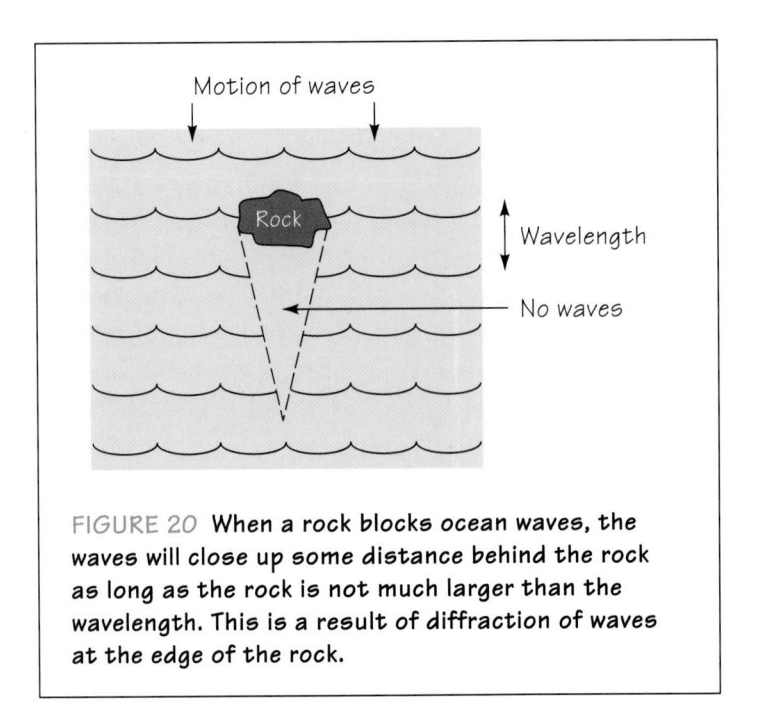

Motion of waves

Rock

Wavelength

No waves

FIGURE 20 **When a rock blocks ocean waves, the waves will close up some distance behind the rock as long as the rock is not much larger than the wavelength. This is a result of diffraction of waves at the edge of the rock.**

page. Notice that the waves close up some distance beyond the rock. For this to happen, the rock must not be much larger than the wavelength (the distance between two adjacent crests of the waves).

The light passing by the edge of any object also bends, but very slightly. The electrons in the molecules at the edge of the object do the bending. The bent or diffracted light that has passed close to the edge interferes with the nondiffracted light a little farther from the edge. This gives a diffraction pattern of light and dark or colored stripes. Experiment 12 explains how you can see this effect for yourself.

# FINGER DIFFRACTION

Close one eye and look at a bright window or at a bare lightbulb. Hold up one hand about 12 inches (30 cm) in front of the open eye. Squeeze your fingers together so that only a very little light comes through between the fingers, as shown in Figure 21. Notice one or two thin dark lines in the light between your fingers as you squeeze your fingers and twist your hand a little. These light and dark lines are the diffraction pattern produced when light is bent by electrons at the edges of your fingers.

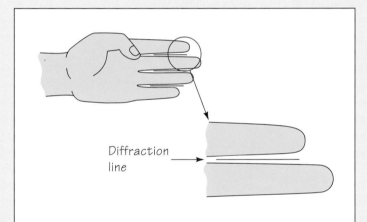

Diffraction line

FIGURE 21 **Close one eye and hold your hand about 12 inches (30 cm) from you. If you look toward a bright light, you will see a diffraction pattern—one or two thin lines—between your fingers.**

When light from the sun or moon passes through a haze or cloud, you may see colored patches or rings. This pattern, called an aureole, is also caused by diffraction. Here light is diffracted from electrons at the edges of tiny particles in the air. (Note that this is *not* the scattering we discussed in Chapter 4, which was caused by particles smaller than the wavelength.) The diffracted light beams from opposite sides of each particle then interfere on their way to our eyes. Colored rings caused by diffraction can be seen from tiny particles that are a little larger than the wavelength of light, but not too large.

Look for an aureole around the sun when there are thin clouds. ***Be careful! Looking directly at the sun can damage your eyes. Wear very dark sunglasses or two pairs of regular sunglasses.*** An aureole looks bluish white near the sun and reddish brown farther out. Additional colors are seen occasionally. Whole clouds or the edges of clouds sometimes show diffraction colors even when they are not close to the sun. Iridescent clouds are most visible when the sun is behind the dark part of a cloud. Their reds, blues, and greens can then be seen through dark sunglasses. Sometimes, an aureole appears around the moon. Since the light from the moon is so weak, we do not see color.

Mountain climbers sometimes see their shadows on a layer or wall of fog. The shadows of their heads can then be surrounded by a *glory*—a set of circular color bands that look like a halo. A glory occurs when light is diffracted by the fog particles. You may see a glory

A glory—a colored circle seen here around the shadow of an airplane—is produced by the interference of light waves diffracted from water droplets in the cloud.

surrounding the shadow of a plane on a cloud if you are seated on the side of the plane away from the sun.

## THE GLORY IN A MIRROR

Place a flashlight on a chair or table so that the light shines down a dark hall or long room. Hold a mirror and stand about 10 feet (3 m) or more away from the flashlight with your back to it. You must be able to see the light from the flashlight reflected in the mirror. Breathe out lightly through your mouth onto the mirror so that the moisture in your breath condenses on the mirror in the form of a fine mist. Quickly look at the flashlight reflected in the misted mirror. You will see the glory as a colored ring around the reflection of the flashlight.

Sometimes you can see the glory at night merely by looking at a distant bright light. The glory may then come from fog or from the dust on a window or windshield. It can even come from tiny scattering particles in your eyes.

### DIFFRACTION GRATINGS

Like multilayer interference, diffraction gives much more intense colors when the colors from many diffracting edges coincide. This can happen when there is a repeating pattern of many equally spaced diffracting lines or dots called a *diffraction grating*. A diffraction grating produces several sets of spectra, either in a row or in a two-dimensional arrangement. Look for such

Colors produced by the interference of light waves scatter from the fine lines on a compact disc. (This photograph shows the colors, but cannot show the iridescence.)

diffraction grating colors from the fine lines on CDs (compact disks) and laser disks.

## DIFFRACTION SPECTRA IN AN UMBRELLA

Again place a flashlight on a chair or table in a dark hall or long room. Stand about 10 feet (3 m) away and open a black or dark-colored cloth umbrella (a plastic one will

69

not work). Look through the fabric at the light. You will see a pattern of tiny spectra diffracted from the two sets of threads in the cloth. You can even take a photograph of this with a telephoto lens. If you can't find a black cloth umbrella, a white cloth handkerchief stretched tight will work, but not quite as well.

The gemstone opal also shows brilliant iridescent colors. Opal contains an ordered arrangement of tiny spheres of a chemical called silica ($SiO_2$). Each sphere is about 250 nm across. These spheres act as a diffraction grating. Look for this gemstone in the window of a jewelry store.

# CHAPTER SIX
## SODIUM YELLOW, BLUE WATER, AND RED-HOT METAL

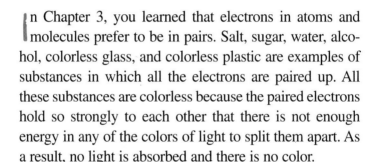

In Chapter 3, you learned that electrons in atoms and molecules prefer to be in pairs. Salt, sugar, water, alcohol, colorless glass, and colorless plastic are examples of substances in which all the electrons are paired up. All these substances are colorless because the paired electrons hold so strongly to each other that there is not enough energy in any of the colors of light to split them apart. As a result, no light is absorbed and there is no color.

Atoms or molecules that have unpaired electrons can absorb some of the wavelengths of white light. When this happens, the substance has color.

Pairs of electrons can become separated when a molecule in a gas is split up into its atoms by high temperature or high voltage. The result is color *gas excitations*. Any substance can produce color as *incandescence* if the temperature is high enough. Sometimes color can involve vibrations and rotations within molecules.

### SODIUM YELLOW GAS EXCITATION
An atom of sodium has one unpaired electron in its outer shell. An atom of chlorine has one electron mis-

sing from its almost full outer shell. When these two atoms combine, the sodium gives its unpaired electron to the chlorine. As a result, all the electrons are paired up in full shells, and the colorless compound sodium chloride (NaCl) forms. This is the table salt we use on our food.

## EXPERIMENT FIFTEEN

## THE SODIUM YELLOW FLAME

Put a few drops of vinegar into a saucer and add a little table salt to make a paste. Stir the mixture for several minutes with the end of a bare copper or iron wire that is at least 4 inches (10 cm) long. Next, hold the wire by its end and carefully touch the wet end of the wire to the lower edge of a pale-blue gas flame or propane-torch flame. Notice the brilliant yellow color of the flame. This yellow color is produced by any material that contains sodium. Other flame colors include the violet of potassium, the green of barium, and the red of lithium, calcium, and strontium.

In Experiment 15, the sodium chloride was split apart by the heat of the flame. Each free sodium atom then had one unpaired electron in its outer shell. The high temperature of the flame gave extra energy to this electron—it "excited" the atom. The excited sodium atom could then lose the extra energy. This energy was given off partly as heat and partly as light. Quantum

When sodium salt is vaporized by the heat of a flame, it emits a yellow color.

theory shows that the excited sodium atom cannot give off just any color light. Most of the light given off by an excited sodium atom has an energy of 2.10 eV. Light of this energy has a wavelength of 589 nm. Thus, gas excitation of sodium produces a yellow light that is usually called "sodium yellow." Chemists can use this type of *flame test* to determine whether sodium is present in a sample of unknown material. Flame tests can also be used to determine whether other elements are present in an unknown substance.

It is also possible to obtain sodium yellow light by using electricity to excite the atoms. A very high voltage is used to do this with miniature lightning flashes in sodium-vapor lamps. These lamps are often used to illuminate highways and parking lots because they give bright sodium yellow light at a very low cost.

## OTHER GAS EXCITATIONS

Sodium is not the only element that emits gas excitation colors under high-voltage conditions. Mercury, the liquid metal used in some glass thermometers, is also used in mercury-vapor lamps. These lamps, sometimes used along highways and in parking lots, give a low-cost bluish light. When excited, mercury atoms give off light at several wavelengths in the visible spectrum as well as in the ultraviolet region of the electromagnetic spectrum.

Fluorescent-tube lamps, which are used in many office buildings and schools, also use mercury excitation. The invisible ultraviolet energy from these lamps is absorbed by a phosphor, a fine powder that is used to coat the inside of the glass wall of the tubes. The phosphor changes the UV into lower-energy visible light, mostly in the orange part of the spectrum, by a process called *fluorescence*. The color given off by fluorescent-tube lamps is between the color of daylight and that of incandescent lightbulbs. Per unit of electricity used, fluorescent-tube lamps emit a white light about five

Sodium-vapor lamps provide intense yellowish light at a low cost.

times brighter than the light given off by incandescent lightbulbs.

Neon tubes, which are widely used in advertising signs, consist of glass tubes filled with neon, helium, or other gases. When excited by electricity, neon gives a red color, while helium emits an orange color. A mixture of helium and neon is used to produce the helium gas excitation responsible for the red laser light (633 nm) given off by a helium-neon laser.

When energetic particles from the sun excite electrons in the atmosphere, we see light of various colors. This phenomenon is known as an aurora.

## GAS EXCITATIONS IN NATURE

Aurora borealis (the northern lights) is seen in the Northern Hemisphere, while aurora australis (the southern lights) can be viewed in the Southern Hemisphere. These natural phenomena have been called nature's neon signs. When huge storms occur at sunspots on the surface of the sun at temperatures of about 10,300°F (5,700°C), large quantities of excited atoms and electrons are released in all directions. When such particles approach our planet, they are concentrated near the north and south magnetic poles by Earth's magnetic field. These particles excite some of the electrons in the atoms and molecules in air in the upper atmosphere. The extra energy is then given off as light of various colors.

Lightning strokes are huge electric sparks from very high voltages built up in clouds. These sparks heat the air so much that light is produced by gas excitations that occur in the air.

## EXPERIMENT SIXTEEN

## CRUNCH AURORA AND ZIP LIGHTNING

You will need some hard wintergreen candy, such as a wintergreen Lifesaver and a roll of masking tape. Stand in front of a mirror in a very dark room for several minutes until your eyes get used to the darkness. Now crunch the candy between your teeth. Notice how your mouth lights up with a blue light. (Be careful not to injure your teeth! It might be safer to crush the candy with a pair of pliers, but then be careful of your fingers!)

Breaking the candy produces electricity, which gives tiny lightning strokes. These "lightning strokes" excite nitrogen molecules in the air to give off a pale-blue light, just like auroras. You can do this experiment with other hard candies, but the light will be weaker. The effect is stronger with wintergreen candy because ultraviolet rays, which are also produced, excite the oil of wintergreen in the candy. The oil of wintergreen responds by giving off a strong blue fluorescence.

Now, unroll your tape very quickly. You should see some weak blue flashes of light. These are caused by gas excitation from tiny electrical sparks (electricity) produced by "unzipping" the adhesive.

## VIBRATIONS AND ROTATIONS

If we take some solid crystals of the black element iodine and heat them gently, an intense violet color appears in the gas above the crystals. The name of this element comes from the Greek word *ioedes,* meaning violet.

Each atom of iodine has a single unpaired electron in its almost full outer shell. Iodine atoms join up in pairs to form iodine molecules. The atoms are held together by the pairing of the one unpaired electron from each of the two atoms. We can picture the iodine molecule as two weights held together with a spring. The spring stands for the bond between the atoms, as in

When iodine is heated, iodine vapor is released. The molecules in the vapor rotate and vibrate. These movements cause color absorption that gives the vapor an intense violet color.

Figure 22a on the next page. Imagine pulling a metal spring attached to two weights so that it vibrates. The two weights move in toward each other, then out away from one another. If we give this molecule a spin, it rotates. See Figure 22b.

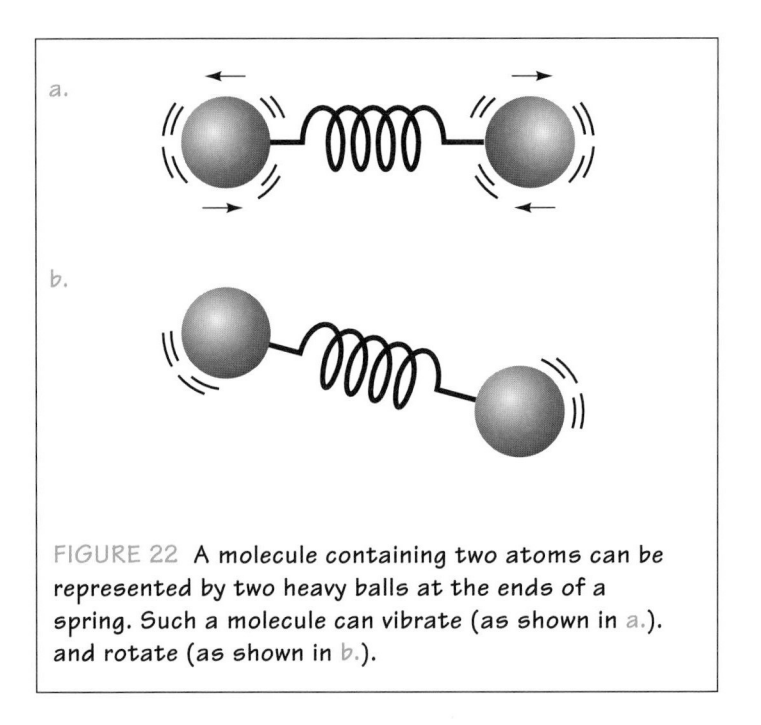

FIGURE 22 A molecule containing two atoms can be represented by two heavy balls at the ends of a spring. Such a molecule can vibrate (as shown in a.). and rotate (as shown in b.).

When white light passes through iodine gas, some of the visible part of the spectrum is absorbed. This causes the electrons in the iodine molecules to become excited and makes the molecules vibrate and rotate. But there is no absorption of light between 450 and 400 nm. As a result, this range of colors is transmitted through the iodine vapor and gives it a beautiful violet color.

We often see other colors where vibrations and rotations are involved. When molecules of water and ice vibrate, they absorb very weakly at the red end of the spectrum. Because the orange-red absorption is so weak, we see color only when we are looking through a large quantity of water or ice. The result is the complementary blue color we see in the water of a clean swimming pool with white walls and white bottom as well as in very clean river or ocean water. The same process gives a pale-blue color to icebergs. The green color sometimes seen in water or ice comes from tiny plants such as green algae.

We know that the blue color of water is not a reflection from the blue of the sky because water remains blue when the sky is white or gray with clouds. However, if there is wind, then the waves, spray, and air bubbles at the surface reflect and scatter light so that we can no longer see the blue color.

In a dark room, look closely at the flame of a candle. You will see a blue area at the bottom of the flame. In this area the partial burning of the wax in the candle flame has made some molecules that survive only a short time before they burn completely. These molecules are excited by the heat of the flame to vibrate and rotate. This, combined with some electron excitation, results in the blue light. You can see the same blue in the flame of a match, in the flame of a kitchen gas range or in a propane-torch flame.

## INCANDESCENCE

The gas excitations, rotations, and vibrations described above give color in atoms or molecules of only a few elements. However, all materials glow with light when they are very hot. Again electrons, atoms, and molecules become excited. At very high temperatures, so many different excitations are possible that the color depends only on the temperature. The colors you see under these conditions are called the incandescence.

Look at a metal poker being heated in a fireplace, the metal element heating up on an electric heater, or a piece of wire held in a gas- or propane-torch flame. As the metal heats up, its color changes from no emitted color or "black" to dark red. If the metal continues to be heated, it will turn brigh red, then orange, and, finally, yellow. If the temperature is high enough, the metal will eventually look white or bluish white, as some stars do.

We use these incandescent colors to describe temperature. We say that something is red-hot, yellow-hot, white-hot, and so on. Table 3 lists the colors associated with various temperatures. There are instruments that can measure temperatures very accurately by measuring these colors.

The yellow light of a candle flame comes from small, hot particles of soot that have been heated to

## TABLE 3 THE COLOR SCALE OF TEMPERATURE

| COLOR | TEMPERATURE |
| --- | --- |
| No color (black) | Below about 500°C (900°F) |
| Barely detectable red | About 500°C (900°F) |
| Dark (cherry) red | About 700°C (1,300°F) |
| Bright red | About 900°C (1,650°F) |
| Orange | About 1,200°C (2,200°F) |
| Yellow | About 1,500°C (2,700°F) |
| White | About 2,500°C to 9,000°C (4,500 to 16,000°F) |
| Bluish white | About 10,000°C (18,000°F) and higher |

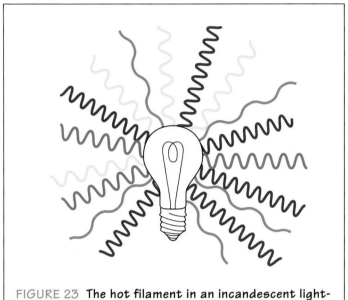

FIGURE 23 **The hot filament in an incandescent light-bulb gives off all colors in all directions.**

about 2,700°F (1,500°C). These soot particles are produced by the partial burning of the wax. When these particles are burned completely in the outer parts of the flame, the result is carbon dioxide ($CO_2$). Look for the soot by *carefully* holding a metal spoon in the upper yellow part of a candle or in a match flame for 2 seconds.

The light given off by an incandescent lightbulb is produced when a wire inside the bulb reaches about 4,000°F (2,200°C). This wire is heated by the flow of electricity and gives off a yellowish-white light that contains some light of every color, as shown in Figure 23.

The temperature of the sun's surface is about 10,300°F (5,700°C). As Newton discovered, the sun gives off the mixture of colors that we see as white. If you think about it, you will realize that daylight is a combination of blue scattered light from the sky and direct sunlight. The sun itself looks yellowish-white because some of its blue has been scattered, as described in Chapter 4. The sun also gives off ultraviolet—from which we get suntans and sunburns—and infrared, which we feel as heat on our skin. Very hot stars in the night sky have a surface temperature of 18,000 to 36,000°F (10,000 to 20,000°C), and look bluish-white to us. No matter how high the temperature, this is the "hottest" color.

As you learned earlier, some of the light from lightning strokes comes from gas excitations. The rest comes from incandescence. The white light and sparks in fireworks also come from incandescence, usually from the burning of magnesium metal powder. Chemicals that give gas-excitation colors are added to create colored fireworks. For example, the high temperature of the burning magnesium excites sodium to give sodium yellow light and strontium to give red light.

# CHAPTER SEVEN
## BLUE JEANS, ORANGE CARROTS, AND GREEN GRASS

**M**ost plant colors and some animal colors are produced by *organic molecules*. Such molecules give the orange color to carrots and the green color to grass and plant leaves. Dyes used to color fabrics and other materials are extracted from plants or synthesized by chemists.

### COLOR IN ORGANIC MOLECULES

Organic molecules make up most of our bodies as well as most of the bodies of animals and plants. Organic molecules contain carbon (C) atoms, usually in the form of chains and rings that are connected to each other. Also present are lots of hydrogen (H) atoms and oxygen (O) atoms as well as smaller quantities of other atoms such as nitrogen (N). Sometimes metal atoms, such as iron (Fe) and magnesium (Mg), are also present.

An example of a color-causing organic molecule is the blue dye called indigo. Indigo, one of the oldest dyes known, was extracted from plants and used to dye clothes 4,000 years ago. It is still used today for coloring some blue jeans. The drawing at the top of Figure

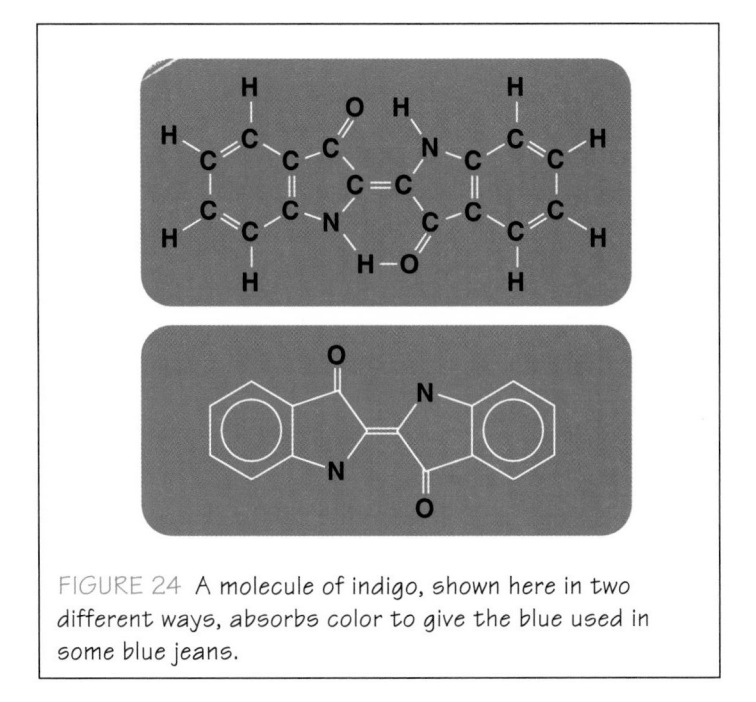

FIGURE 24 A molecule of indigo, shown here in two different ways, absorbs color to give the blue used in some blue jeans.

24 shows a molecule of indigo with all of its atoms and bonds. Each line indicates a bond formed by a pair of electrons. The indigo molecule is shown in its simplest form (with all carbon atoms and hydrogen atoms left out) at the bottom of Figure 24. To a chemist, these two drawings mean exactly the same thing.

Other organic color-producing molecules found in plants are the orange *beta-carotene* of carrots (Figure 25a) and the green chlorophyll of grass and other plant leaves (Figure 25b). The red *heme* molecule (Figure 25c) is an important part of the cells that give our blood its red color. These red blood cells carry oxygen from the lungs to the rest of the body. It is interesting to note that chlorophyll, one of the most important molecules

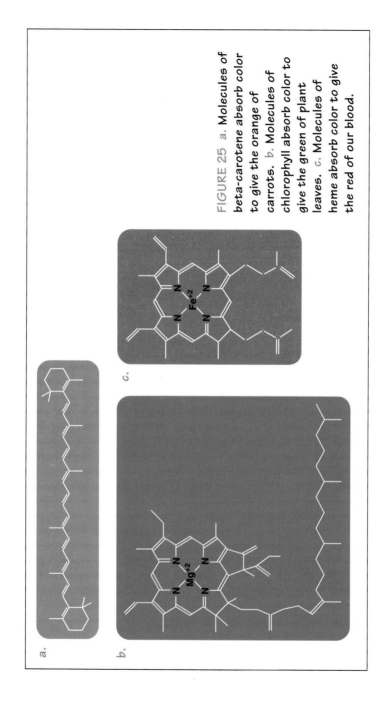

FIGURE 25 a. Molecules of beta-carotene absorb color to give the orange of carrots. b. Molecules of chlorophyll absorb color to give the green of plant leaves. c. Molecules of heme absorb color to give the red of our blood.

a.

b.

c.

in plants, and heme, one of the most important molecules in animals, have different colors but similar shapes.

The chains and rings of carbon atoms in organic molecules are often connected with alternating single and double carbon-carbon bonds. In a *single bond*, one unpaired electron from each of two carbon atoms is shared to form a pair. This holds the atoms together and gives $C-C$. In a *double bond*, two unpaired electrons are shared by the two carbon atoms, giving $C=C$. Both kinds are shown in Figures 24 and 25.

In large organic molecules, some of these paired electrons can move around on alternating single and double bonds. When this happens, the electrons can absorb light and become excited. However, not all the colors in white light are absorbed. The electrons in chlorophyll absorb blue and violet light. They also absorb yellow, orange, and red light. Only green light is not absorbed. This green light is reflected from and transmitted through the leaves of plants, giving them their green color.

Both science and art are needed to create the many organic pigments and dyes that chemists invent for coloring fabrics for our clothes, inks for writing and printing, and cosmetics such as lipstick, nail polish, and hair dye. Some dyes fade when exposed to light, ultraviolet, or even to pollution in the air.

## COLOR CHANGES IN FOOD

The organic molecules in foods have interesting color changes. Tomatoes turn red and become tasty as they ripen on the plants. The chemical changes of the ripening process produce both the red pigments and the sugars. Tomatoes shipped over long distances are often picked when they are green and ripened by being exposed to ethylene gas. While this process produces the pigments that make the tomatoes look red, it does not produce the sugars, so the good taste is missing.

The color of most foods is not changed by cooking or by other food ingredients. Carrots stay orange, tomatoes stay red, and egg yolks stay yellow. Some foods do change color, however. For example, a lobster's shell turns red when it is boiled, and apples and eggplant change color when they are exposed to oxygen in the air.

## EXPERIMENT SEVENTEEN

## COLOR CHANGES IN FOODS

- Take some fresh (not frozen) green beans or broccoli pieces and watch closely as you put them into a pot of boiling water. Notice how they quickly turn a brighter green but then go back to their original color after a few minutes. Now add a little vinegar and boil them for a few more minutes. The acid in the vinegar removes magnesium (Mg) from the chlorophyll, and the result is an unappetizing color change.

- Put a little cooked red cabbage into each of two glasses. Add 1 teaspoon of vinegar or lemon juice, which are acids, to one glass and a ¼ teaspoon of baking soda, which is alkaline (the opposite of acid), to the other. What happens to the color of the cabbage? Slowly and carefully add some vinegar or lemon juice to the glass with the baking soda. (It will foam.) When you have added enough acid to neutralize the alkali, you will see the color change.

- Boil a few strawberries, blackberries, raspberries, or blueberries with ½ cup of water for a few minutes. Squash the fruit with a spoon so that the juices are released into the water. After the water has cooled, pour some into two glasses. Add a few drops of vinegar or lemon juice to one glass and sprinkle a little baking soda into the other. You will see a color difference. Again try neutralization. You can also try this with grape juice.

- Mix a little vinegar, lemon juice, or vitamin C powder with a few drops of water. (All are acid substances.) Cut two small pieces of a freshly peeled apple, pear, or banana. Dip one of the pieces into the acid mixture. After a few hours, you will see that the uncoated fruit has turned brown from reacting with the oxygen in the air. The fruit dipped in acid will not turn brown.

# CHAPTER EIGHT

## THE STATUE OF LIBERTY, RUBY, SMOKY QUARTZ, AND FOOL'S GOLD

When the metal copper (Cu) is exposed to weather, the acids and other pollutants in rain slowly eat at the surface of the copper and give it a thin skin of copper compounds. The Statue of Liberty originally had the shiny reddish color of copper. Over the last hundred years, a green coat of copper *patina* has formed on its surface. This green color is caused by unpaired electrons in compounds of copper, which is a *transition metal.* Even a small amount of a transition metal compound can produce an intense color, as in the gemstone ruby.

### TRANSITION METAL COMPOUNDS

The atoms of some metals, such as copper, iron, chromium, manganese, and cobalt, have unpaired electrons in their outermost shells as well as unpaired electrons in an inner shell. When the outermost unpaired electrons pair up to form compounds, the inner unpaired electrons may remain unpaired. Chemists call elements that have unfilled inner shells "transition metals."

In Chapter 6, you saw that unpaired electrons in the outer shell of a sodium atom can absorb energy and become excited. Unpaired electrons in the inner shell of a transition metal in a molecule can also be excited by absorbing energy from *quanta* of light. Since only some energies can be absorbed, the light that remains is no longer white. This process gives the green patina to the Statue of Liberty. Copper patina consists of a mixture of molecules containing copper along with sulfate ($SO_4$), chloride ($Cl_2$), carbonate ($CO_3$), hydroxide (OH), and water molecules.

Some minerals and gems have color because they are transition metal compounds. One example is turquoise, the blue-to-green copper-containing gemstone widely used in Native American jewelry. Transition metals have intense colors. Several are used as pigments in paints, as in the chromium pigment chrome green ($Cr_2O_3$) and the cobalt pigment cobalt blue ($CoAl_2O_4$).

## TRANSITION METAL IMPURITIES

A material that is colorless when pure can become colored when it contains just a few transition metal atoms for every 100 other atoms. These transition metal atoms are usually called the "impurity" in the "host" material.

Only 1 or 2 chromium impurity atoms for every 100 host atoms are required to transform the colorless beryl ($Be_3Al_2Si_6O_{18}$) into the gemstone emerald. Emerald has a beautiful green color. If you shine ultraviolet onto an emerald, it glows red. The ultraviolet excites the unpaired inner electrons and some of this energy is emitted as a red fluorescence.

When beryl contains a small amount of chromium, it looks green and is called emerald.

What do you think happens when the colorless host corundum ($Al_2O_3$) contains the same amount of the chromium impurity that transforms colorless beryl into a stunning green emerald? The answer may surprise you. The result is ruby, a beautiful deep-red gemstone. The way the unpaired electrons in chromium absorb light has been changed by the host. Although the

When corundum contains a small amount of chromium,
it looks red and is called ruby.

chromium atoms absorb light differently, exposing a
ruby to ultraviolet produces the same red fluorescence
in a ruby as in an emerald. The ruby fluorescence,
which is very strong (694 nm, 1.787 eV), is used to
obtain the ruby laser's red beam.

In a very rare gemstone called alexandrite, the colorless host chrysoberyl ($BeAl_2O_4$) contains a chromium

The chromium impurity in the gemstone alexandrite causes it to look greenish in daylight (above) and reddish in incandescent light (below).

impurity that behaves halfway between the way it acts in emerald and the way it acts in ruby. It is hard to believe, but both green and red colors can be seen in alexandrite! In daylight (or in the light from a fluorescent-tube lamp) alexandrite looks green. In candlelight or light emitted by an incandescent lightbulb, alexandrite looks red.

Some transition metal impurities are used to color glass. An iron impurity called ferrous iron ($Fe^{2+}$) has unpaired inner electrons. When these electrons absorb some light, they produce the green color seen in many bottles. A small amount of this iron is often present as an impurity in the chemicals used to make colorless glass. The result is a pale-green color.

In some cases, manganese is added to get rid of this pale-green color. Manganese is also a transition metal with unpaired inner electrons. These electrons absorb light to give glass a pale-purple color. Since purple and green are complementary colors, as you learned in Chapter 2, the green-producing absorptions of the iron and the purple-producing absorptions of the manganese balance each other, so that the glass appears to have no color. The resulting glass is a little darker than pure colorless glass, which does not absorb any light.

### SMOKY QUARTZ AND AMETHYST

Colorless quartz, sometimes called rock crystal, is often found in the ground. Quartz consists of silicon oxide ($SiO_2$) and usually contains a small amount of aluminum (Al) as an impurity (about 1 aluminum atom for every 1,000 host atoms). Both the quartz host and the aluminum impurity have only paired electrons. Therefore this quartz absorbs no light and is colorless.

Smoky quartz, sometimes used as a gemstone, has a brown to black color. Smoky quartz contains exactly the same amount of silicon oxide and aluminum as colorless quartz and nothing else. So what causes the smoky color?

Smoky quartz contains an aluminum impurity. When this material was irradiated in nature, the impurity formed a color center, which gives this gemstone its smoky color.

We get a clue when we heat smoky quartz to about 840°F (450°C). Within a few minutes, the color disappears. But if the quartz is exposed to high-energy radiation or particles, the smoky color soon returns. Scientists who have studied the areas where smoky quartz is found, have noticed that there is always some natural radioactive material in the ground. When particles emitted by this radioactive material smash into the aluminum within the quartz, the aluminum is left with an unpaired electron. This unpaired electron is called a *color center* because it absorbs light and is responsible for the color that you see when you look at a piece of smoky quartz. Just 1 color center for every 1,000 to 10,000 atoms is enough to give intense color.

Quartz is also found in a purple form called amethyst, which is used as a gemstone. Amethyst turns yellow on being heated and is then called citrine, which is also a gemstone. Exposure to radiation transforms yellow citrine back to purple amethyst. Citrine contains a kind of iron impurity called ferric iron ($Fe^{3+}$), which has unpaired inner electrons. These electrons absorb violet light and give the complementary yellow color.

A different purple color is seen in desert amethyst glass. This color may develop in old glass bottles that were originally very pale-green (due to ferrous iron impurity) but manganese (Mn) was added to remove the color. In the western desert regions of the United States the air is clear and the ultraviolet rays from the sun are strong. If these glass bottles lie under the desert

Amethyst, a purple quartz gemstone (left), contains a color center based on ferric iron. On being heated, amethyst turns into yellow citrine (right). This change can be reversed by irradiation.

sun for several years, the ultraviolet rays may produce manganese color centers in the glass. These color centers absorb light and give a color similar to that of amethyst. Of course it is much quicker to take one of these old colorless bottles and expose it to radiation in the laboratory for half an hour. The result is the same.

Most types of color centers are not changed by light, but a few do fade. A color center that fades is used in self-darkening sunglasses. The ultraviolet in strong sunlight produces color centers in the glass faster than they can fade. As a result, the sunglasses absorb light to protect our eyes. The dark color fades back to colorless when the light is weaker and contains only a little ultraviolet.

## ELECTRON-HOPPING COLORS

An unusual thing can happen between one transition metal atom and another transition metal atom. Color can result when an electron hops from one atom to another in a process called *electron hopping*. Electron hopping is also called *charge transfer*. Just 1 atom of impurity for every 1,000 atoms of the host is enough to give strong electron-hopping colors.

A brown bottle is made of glass that contains some ferrous iron ($Fe^{2+}$). As you learned earlier, ferrous iron has unpaired inner electrons and absorbs light to give a green color to glass. To make the glass brown, some sulfur is added. The sulfur removes an electron from some of the ferrous iron ($Fe^{2+}$), so that ferric iron ($Fe^{3+}$) forms. Ferric iron also has unpaired inner electrons. By itself, it gives glass that is a pale-yellow color.

When ferrous and ferric iron are present together, light can give its energy to an unpaired electron on a ferric iron so that it hops to a ferrous iron. When the electron hops, the ferric iron becomes a ferrous iron at the same time that the ferrous iron becomes a ferric iron. The light that produces this hopping is absorbed and gives a dark-brown color to the glass.

Other examples of ferrous-ferric electron hopping are the red-brown rust on iron (an iron oxide hydroxide), the deep-blue paint pigment Prussian blue $(Fe_4[Fe(CN)_6]_3 \cdot 12H_2O)$, and the yellow to brown iron-containing paint pigments ocher, sienna, and umber. Most of the colors in sandstone and other rocks of the Painted Desert of Arizona are also the result of ferrous-ferric electron hopping.

If the colorless host corundum contains 1 ferrous iron impurity for every 1,000 host atoms, the result is a very pale-yellow color. If it contains 1 titanium impurity for every 1,000 host atoms, there is no color at all. However, if both iron and titanium are present, the result is the intense blue color of sapphire.

Both ferrous iron and titanium have unpaired inner electrons. In blue sapphire, the energy of yellow light is absorbed as an electron hops from the iron to the titanium, producing the deep-blue color that is complementary to the yellow absorption. This same iron-titanium electron hopping gives a gray-to-black color to the rocks that astronauts brought back from the moon.

If you have ever gone rock hunting, you may have found some yellow sparkling pyrite $(FeS_2)$. Pyrite is also called fool's gold because it looks just like gold and sometimes fools miners. You can tell them apart quite easily, however, because a pocket knife will cut into the gold, but it will cause pyrite to crumble. (Do *not* try this test on your mother's gold jewelry!) Fool's

The colors of rocks in the Painted Desert of Arizona are the result of electron hopping between ferrous iron and ferric iron impurities.

gold contains both iron and sulfur. An electron hopping from a sulfur to an iron absorbs blue light and gives pyrite its complementary goldlike yellow color. Unusual conditions also give it a metallic appearance. In a similar way, the electrons hop from oxygen to chromium in the deep-yellow paint pigment chrome yellow ($PbCrO_4$).

# CHAPTER NINE
## GOLD, VERMILION, THE HOPE DIAMOND, AND LEDs

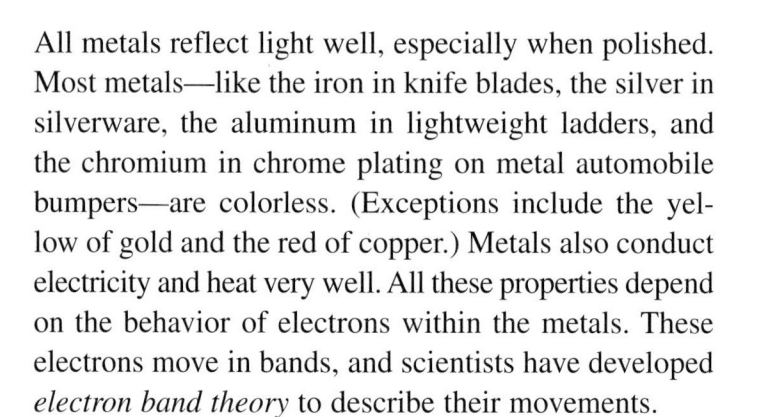

All metals reflect light well, especially when polished. Most metals—like the iron in knife blades, the silver in silverware, the aluminum in lightweight ladders, and the chromium in chrome plating on metal automobile bumpers—are colorless. (Exceptions include the yellow of gold and the red of copper.) Metals also conduct electricity and heat very well. All these properties depend on the behavior of electrons within the metals. These electrons move in bands, and scientists have developed *electron band theory* to describe their movements.

These same movable electrons are at work in *semiconductors*, where they give us intensely colored pigments such as vermilion, gemstones such as the famous Hope diamond, light-emitting diodes (LEDs), and semiconductor lasers.

### METALS AND ALLOYS

As you learned in Chapter 3, unpaired electrons in the outer shell of an atom are involved in forming molecules. Although these electrons usually remain on the atoms or on the molecules, they can move around within the molecule in some organic molecules. In a metal, however, the outer unpaired electrons can move freely within the entire substance. In 1 cubic centimeter of copper, there are 59 thousand billion billion ($5.9 \times 10^{22}$) atoms and an equal number of movable electrons! These movable electrons can carry electricity and heat along a copper wire. At room temperature, a piece of copper—or any other metal—feels much colder than a piece of wood or plastic because the movable electrons in the metal carry more heat away from the hand. Check it out.

Since some electrons are free to move in a metal, they should be able to absorb light of any energy. In reality, however, metal is a good conductor. Because of this, the electrons in a metal cannot hold on to the energy of a photon. Instead, they re-emit photons immediately, at exactly the same energy. This explains why metals reflect light well and why polished metals are shiny.

Mirrors take advantage of this property of metals. They are made of a sheet of glass with a thin coating of aluminum on the back. The aluminum is then covered with a protective layer of paint. Look for this by *carefully* using a knife to scrape away the back of an old or broken mirror.

Band theory explains the behavior of metals by showing that the electrons move about in an *electron band*. This band describes the energies available to the movable electrons and tells us how many electrons there can be at any energy. Figure 26 on the next page shows how electrons fill up the lower energy of an electron band. An electron in the filled part of a band can

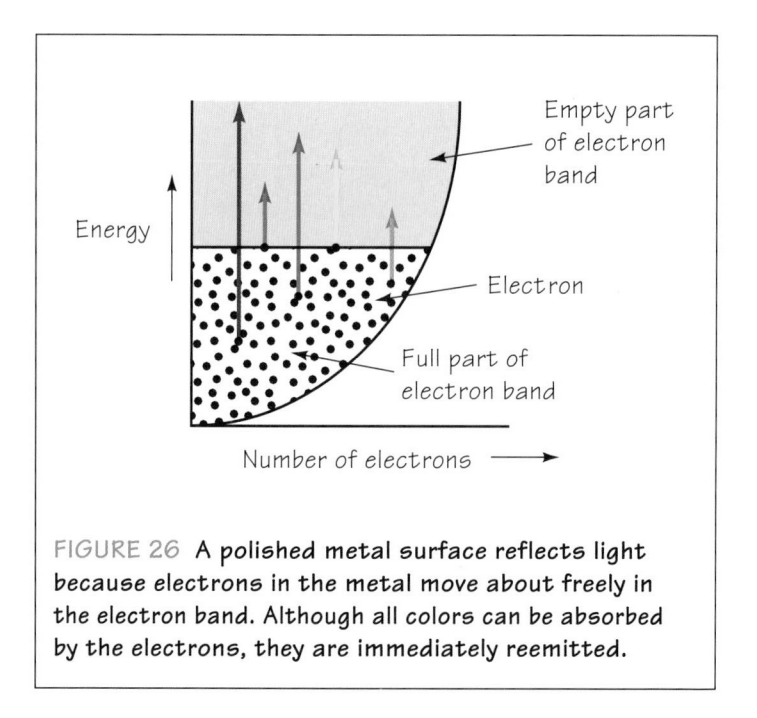

Empty part
of electron
band

Energy

Electron

Full part of
electron band

Number of electrons ⟶

FIGURE 26 A polished metal surface reflects light
because electrons in the metal move about freely in
the electron band. Although all colors can be absorbed
by the electrons, they are immediately reemitted.

absorb light by moving to a higher energy in the empty part of the band. As the light is reflected from the metal surface, the electron loses energy and returns to the lower band.

Some metals, such as gold and copper, can absorb a little of the light at the high-energy end of the spectrum. This absorption of blue and violet light is responsible for the yellow we see when we look at gold, and the red we see when we look at copper. Remember, red and yellow are complementary to blue and violet.

An *alloy* is a mixture of two or more metals, and everything we have said about metals applies equally to alloys. An example of an alloy is the yellow brass often used for doorknobs, which is a mixture of the metals copper and zinc.

## PURE SEMICONDUCTORS

In a few very special materials, called semiconductors, a gap called the *band gap* can appear in the electron band, as shown in Figure 27. Electrons cannot exist at energies inside this gap. The size of the band gap is actually an amount of energy and is measured in electron volt (eV) units (described in Chapter 3). In most cases, the band below the gap is completely full of electrons and the band above the gap is empty. Since these are not good conductors of electricity, they can absorb light and usually do not have the excellent reflection of metals.

First, let us investigate a semiconductor material with a small band gap (less than 1.771 eV). In Chapter

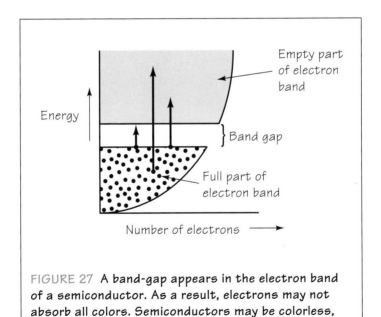

FIGURE 27 **A band-gap appears in the electron band of a semiconductor. As a result, electrons may not absorb all colors. Semiconductors may be colorless, yellow, orange, red, or black.**

3, you learned that this is the lowest energy of any color light that humans can see. Therefore, all the colors in white light can excite electrons across a small band gap and are absorbed. As a result, small band gap semiconductors such as silicon (band gap = 1.10 eV) look dark gray to black.

Now consider a medium band gap semiconductor with a band gap of 2.00 eV. Here the colors with energies less than 2.00 eV—including 1.771 eV (700 nm) red and 1.909 eV (650 nm) reddish orange (see the table in Chapter 3) cannot be absorbed because these energies would excite electrons into the band gap, where they cannot exist. But all higher-energy colors are absorbed because they can excite electrons across the band gap. So only red and red-orange light is reflected or transmitted but other colors are absorbed. An example of such a material is the bright-red mineral cinnabar (HgS), which is also used as a paint pigment called vermilion.

In the same way, a medium band gap semiconductor with a band gap of about 2.30 eV can absorb the colors green, blue, and violet, leaving yellow, orange, and red to be transmitted or reflected. The result is an orange color. One example is the paint pigment cadmium orange ($Cd_2SSe$). At a band gap of 2.60 eV, only violet and some blue are absorbed, leaving the complementary color (yellow) to be transmitted or reflected. This happens in the yellow mineral greenockite (CdS), which is also used as a paint pigment called cadmium yellow.

Finally, what happens in a semiconductor when the band gap is larger than the energy of any color of the spectrum—that is, when the band gap is equal to or larger than the 3.10 eV (400 nm) of violet light? Now there is not enough energy at any color to take electrons across the band gap so the electrons cannot absorb any visible light and white light is reflected or transmitted. An example of such a large band gap semiconductor is the paint pigment zinc-white (ZnO) with a band gap of 3.10 eV. Another example is the gemstone diamond (band gap = 4.60 eV), a very hard form of carbon that is colorless when pure.

## DOPED SEMICONDUCTORS

A colorless large band gap semiconductor may be colored by impurities called *dopants*. An unusual example is the famous Hope diamond, an impressive gem on display at the Smithsonian Institution Museum in Washington, D.C. This diamond contains about 1

In addition to carbon, the Hope diamond contains a tiny amount of boron. This boron impurity produces an energy level in the band gap and absorbs some colors to give an intense blue.

boron atom for every 100,000 carbon atoms. The boron atoms give the Hope diamond its brilliant blue color. If, instead of boron, a diamond contains about the same number of nitrogen atoms, then it has a bright yellow color. Such intensely colored diamonds are extremely rare.

A nitrogen dopant atom has one more electron than the carbon atom it replaces. When a diamond is doped with nitrogen, there is no room for the one extra electron from each nitrogen atom in the electron band below the gap. As a result, each extra electron from nitrogen must enter a dopant energy level inside the band gap, as shown in Figure 28. The energy of blue

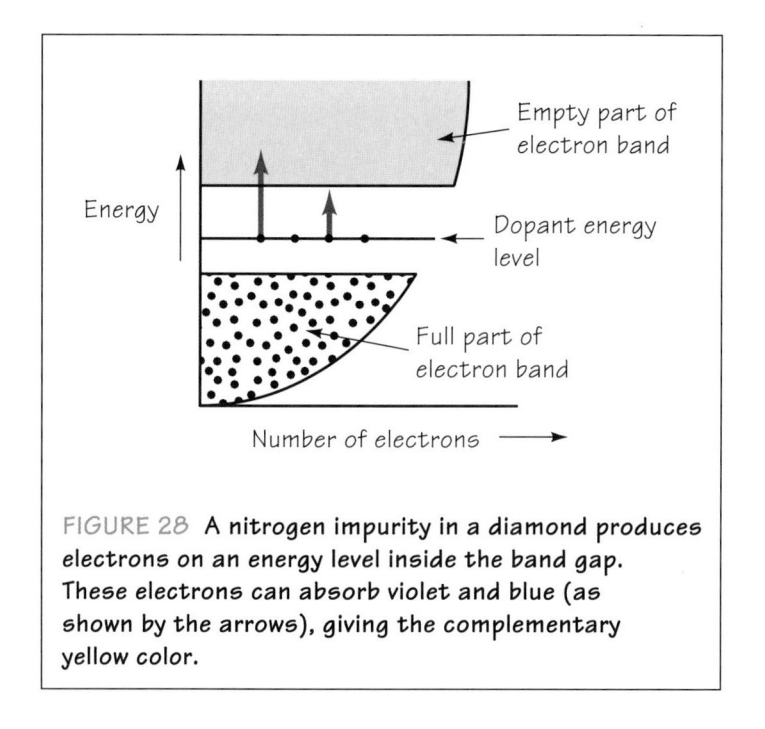

FIGURE 28 A nitrogen impurity in a diamond produces electrons on an energy level inside the band gap. These electrons can absorb violet and blue (as shown by the arrows), giving the complementary yellow color.

and violet light is absorbed by exciting one of the extra dopant electrons out of the band gap. As a result, the nitrogen-doped diamond is yellow, the complementary color of the absorbed light.

A dopant boron atom in the Hope diamond has one less electron than the carbon atom it replaces. These boron atoms form a different type of dopant energy level in the band gap. As a result, electrons absorb yellow light and the diamond looks blue. (Blue and yellow are complementary colors.)

Dopants change the electrical properties in a small band gap semiconductor material, such as silicon, in a very special way. Doped silicon is used in the transistors and integrated circuits of radios, television sets, video recorders, and all the wonderful gadgets of our electronic age. Some of these doped semiconductors emit colored light when electricity is passed through them. This gives us the LEDs you can see in the red displays on many television sets and electronic instruments. It also gives us the semiconductor lasers used in CD (compact disc) and laser disc players.

Doped semiconductors are also used in a powder form called *phosphors*. As mentioned in Chapter 6, phosphors inside fluorescent light tubes convert the ultraviolet emitted from mercury gas excitations into visible light. As discussed in Chapter 2, three phosphors emitting the three additive primaries inside television screens give us a full-color picture. Some phosphor powders give off blue or green light when excited by electricity. These are used in displays on electronic instruments and in the greenish light-emitting panels used in night-lights.

# EPILOGUE
## THE MANY WONDERS OF COLOR

Our ability to see color gives us a great deal of information about the world around us. It adds beauty to our lives and gives us wonder and pleasure that is intensified when we understand how colors are created. While 1 in 20 males and 1 in 200 females have some defects in their color vision, most of these people can still see some colors.

Starting with Newton's prism experiments in 1666, scientists have continued to study and make discoveries about light and color. There have been many surprises since Newton's first insight into color. One example is the unexpected double nature of light, which shows both particle and wave properties, as discussed in Chapter 3. Only with the advent of the quantum theory has the curious nature of light been explained.

Then there is the complexity of the color-vision process and its defects, a subject briefly discussed in Chapter 3. Here our understanding is far from complete and new discoveries are still being made.

The difference between additive and subtractive color mixing and the different sets of primary colors covered in Chapter 2 continue to surprise us, no matter how well we understand them. Although not very complicated, you will find that they are still not widely recognized.

You have learned about many different causes of color in this book, and you may be wondering whether there is a limit to the number of ways that color can be produced. Actually, there are only fifteen ways. These fifteen basic causes are summarized in Table 4.

## TABLE 4 THE FIFTEEN CAUSES OF COLOR

| CAUSE | EXAMPLE | CHAPTER |
|---|---|---|
| Dispersion | Rainbow | 1 |
| Scattering | Blue sky | 4 |
| Interference | Soap-bubble colors | 5 |
| Diffraction | Diffraction grating | 5 |
| Gas excitation | Sodium yellow light | 6 |
| Vibrations and rotations | Blue water | 6 |
| Incandescence | Yellow candle flame | 6 |
| Organic materials | Blue jeans | 7 |
| Transition metal compounds | Statue of Liberty patina | 8 |
| Transition metal impurities | Ruby gemstone | 8 |
| Color centers | Smoky quartz gemstone | 8 |
| Electron hopping | Fool's gold (pyrite) | 8 |
| Metals and alloys | Gold | 9 |
| Pure semiconductors | Pigment vermilion | 9 |
| Doped semiconductors | Hope diamond | 9 |

When you see color or light, you are almost always seeing electrons at work. Electrons are present in all matter. They are so tiny that it takes more than 1 billion billion billion of them to weigh 1 gram. When light passes through matter, electrons slow it down. As you saw in Chapter 1, the result is the refraction and dispersion that permit a prism to spread out the colors present in white light. This effect explains how drops of water form a rainbow. When light is scattered to give blue colors, as described in Chapter 4, it is electrons that do the scattering. And electrons are involved in almost all other causes of color.

Understanding these processes completely requires some knowledge of physics, chemistry, and biology. The books listed in the bibliography can help you learn even more about light and color.

# GLOSSARY

*achromatic color*—any shade without color, such as white, gray, black.

*additive color mixing*—mixing colored light beams or light reflected from adjacent spots of color. It is possible to create almost all visible colors by additive color mixing of red, green, and blue.

*additive primary colors*—red, green, and blue; the colors from which almost all others can be derived by additive color mixing.

*alloy*—a solid or liquid mixture of two or more metals.

*band gap*—a range of electron energies missing in an electron band. This gap determines the color that you see when you look at a semiconductor.

*beta-carotene*—the molecule responsible for the orange color you see when you look at carrots and some other vegetables, fruits, and plants.

*charge transfer*—when an electron "hops" from one atom to another, its negative charge is transferred. This process affects the colors you see when you look at some objects. (See *electron hopping.*)

*chlorophyll*—the magnesium-containing molecule responsible for the green color you see when you look at grass and other plants.

*chromaticity diagram*—another term for a color triangle.

*color center*—when one electron is knocked out of an electron pair in a colorless material, the material can become colored.

*color triangle*—the triangular arrangement of all visible colors at one level of brightness.

*complementary colors*—two colors that are exactly opposite from one another in a color triangle. When two complementary colors are mixed in the proper proportions, the result is white. Blue and yellow are complementary colors, for example.

*cyan*—a bluish green; one of the three subtractive primary colors.

*diffraction*—the bending or spreading of light by the edges of an object.

*diffraction grating*—an object that contains many fine

lines or spots. When white light travels through (or is reflected from) a diffraction grating, the result is a spectrum.

*dispersion*—the separation of light into spectral colors by refraction of light.

*dopant*—a small amount of impurity added to a semiconductor to change its color and/or its electrical properties.

*double bond*—a bond in which two pairs of electrons are shared by two atoms

*dye*—a liquid (or soluble substance) used to color materials such as cloth.

*electromagnetic spectrum*—the total range of electromagnetic radiation, ranging from the longest wavelength radio waves to the shortest gamma rays. The electromagnetic spectrum also includes ultraviolet and infrared energy, visible light, X rays, and microwaves.

*electron*—the tiny particle that carries the smallest negative electrical charge and is present in all atoms. It is also the carrier of electricity. Electrons in atoms and molecules prefer to exist in full electron shells.

*electron band theory*—describes the characteristics of electrons in metals and semiconductors. When electrons move within these materials, they may produce color.

*electron hopping*—the process by which an electron associated with one element moves to another element temporarily. This can produce color. (See *charge transfer.*)

*electron shell*—the electrons in an atom occur in shells, which can hold a limited number of electrons. Electrons in the outer shell may move from one atom to another in an effort to fill these shells in pairs.

*electron volt*—a unit of energy used to describe the photons that are responsible for spectral colors.

*flame test*—a test in which a material is passed through a flame. It is sometimes possible to identify the components of the material by the color of the flame.

*fluorescence*—color produced when electromagnetic energy, such as ultraviolet, is absorbed by a substance and a part of this energy is emitted as visible light.

*gas excitation*—color produced when certain gases or vapors are excited by electricity. Examples include auroras and sodium-vapor lamps.

*glory*—a halo of circular bands of color produced by diffraction.

*hue*—one of three units used to describe light. The term is used to distinguish the subtle differences between different colors or shades of the same color.

*incandescence*—the glow of light from a hot object, such as the filament in a lightbulb.

*infrared (IR)*—an invisible part of the electromagnetic spectrum. It is located just beyond the red portion of the visible spectrum.

*interference*—the combination or cancellation of two light waves of exactly the same wavelength. This effect may cause color, as in a soap bubble.

*iridescence*—intense reflected rainbow-like colors that resemble the reflection of light from metals. This effect is often the result of interference.

*lightness*—one of three units used to describe color. It is generally used to describe the intensity of light.

*magenta*—a reddish-purple; one of the subtractive primary colors.

*metamers/metameric mixtures*—two colors that match perfectly in one type of lighting but do not match under a different lighting because they absorb light differently.

*molecule*—a stable combination of atoms that forms when electrons from one atom are transferred to or shared with another atom. It is the smallest unit of a compound, just as an atom is the smallest unit of an element.

*monochromatic spectral color*—a color composed of only one spectral wavelength.

*nanometer (nm)*—a unit used to measure wavelengths of light. 1 nanometer = 1/1,000,000,000 meter (one-billionth of a meter).

*non spectral color*—a color that does not occur in the spectrum. Examples include brown, olive, and pink.

*organic molecule*—a carbon-based molecule, which may also include hydrogen, oxygen, nitrogen, and other elements. All living organisms are composed of organic molecules.

*patina*—a green coat formed on the surface of copper by corrosion. The color originates in unpaired electrons.

*phosphor*—a powder that fluoresces. It usually consists of a doped semiconductor.

*photon*—the smallest indivisible quantity of light in any part of the visible spectrum. It can be described by its energy in electron volts or by its wavelength.

*pigment*—a fine powder that gives paint its color.

*primary color*—one of several sets of three or four colors used in additive and subtractive color mixing to produce almost all colors.

*quantum/quanta (pl.)*—the smallest indivisible quantity of energy in any part of the electromagnetic spectrum. A quantum can be described by its energy in electron volts or by its wavelength. A quantum in the visible-light region of the electromagnetic spectrum may also be called a photon.

*quantum theory*—the study of energy and other properties of quanta, photons, electrons, atoms, and molecules.

*reflection*—the bending aside or turning back of light. Light may be reflected by a mirror or a piece of white paper.

*refraction*—the bending of light as it enters or exits a transparent substance, such as glass.

*refractive index (RI)*—a measure of the amount of refraction produced by a transparent substance.

*saturated color*—a spectral color that is pure or vivid and is not mixed with white, gray, or black. Saturated colors occur at the edges of the color triangle.

*saturation*—one of three units used to describe color. It describes a color's degree of purity. It is greatest for saturated colors at the edge of the color triangle and decreases as white, gray, or black is added.

*scattering*—(a) the effect observed when a rough surface or powdered substance throws white light in all directions and no color change occurs; (b) the effect observed when molecules or dust in the air throw some colors of light in all directions. This type of scattering is strongest at the violet end of the spectrum and gives color. The blue of the sky and the red of a sunset are the result of scattering.

*semiconductor*—a substance that conducts electricity better than an insulator but not as well as a metal.

*single bond*—a bond in which a pair of electrons are shared by two atoms.

*spectral color*—the range of colors that fall within the visible-light region of the electromagnetic spectrum (red, orange, yellow, green, blue, violet, and all intermediate colors). The spectral colors can be seen in a rainbow.

*spectrum/spectra (pl.)*—the name Newton gave to the visible sequence of colors in the visible-light region of the electromagnetic spectrum.

*subtractive color mixing*—mixing colored paints, pigments, or dyes to obtain almost all visible colors by absorption.

*subtractive primary colors*—yellow, magenta, and cyan; the colors from which almost all others can be derived by subtractive color mixing.

*transition metal*—a metal that contains unpaired electrons in an inner electron shell.

*ultraviolet (UV)*—the invisible part of the electromagnetic spectrum located just beyond violet.

*unsaturated color*—a color that is mixed with some white, gray, or black and occurs toward the center of the color triangle.

*wavelength*—the distance between two adjacent crests in a wave. For light, wavelengths are usually expressed in units called nanometers (nm).

# FOR FURTHER READING

Gardner, Robert. *Experimenting with Light*. New York: Franklin Watts, 1991.

Greenler, Robert. *Rainbows, Halos, and Glories*. New York: Cambridge University Press, 1980.

Minnaert, M. *The Nature of Light and Color*. New York: Dover, 1954.

Zwimpfer, Morris. *Color, Light, Sight, Sense: An Elementary Theory of Color in Pictures*. West Chester, PA: Schiffer Publishing Ltd., 1988.

***MORE-ADVANCED BOOKS***
Falk, David S., Dieter R. Brill, and David G. Stork. *Seeing the Light: Optics in Nature, Photography, Color Vision, and Holography*. New York: John Wiley and Sons, 1986.

Lynch, David K., and William Livingstone. *Color and Light in Nature*. New York: Cambridge University Press, 1995.

Nassau, Kurt. *The Physics and Chemistry of Color*. New York: John Wiley and Sons, 1983.

Overheim, R. Daniel, and David L. Wagner. *Light and Color*. New York: John Wiley and Sons, 1982.

Williamson, Samuel J., and Herman Z. Cummins. *Light and Color in Nature and Art*. New York: John Wiley and Sons, 1983.

# INDEX

# ABOUT THE AUTHOR

Kurt Nassau recently retired as Distinguished Research Scientist after 30 years at AT&T Bell Laboratories. He worked on projects that involved laser materials, color, crystals, and glasses. He has a Ph.D. from the University of Pittsburgh. Dr. Nassau has written five books and many articles, including one called "Colour," which has appeared in the *Encyclopædia Britannica* since 1988. He has taught at Princeton University and frequently gives lectures at universities, colleges, and high schools.